THE DARK SIDE OF
GAME TEXTURING

THOMSON

OURSE TECHNOLOGY

ofessional ■ Trade ■ Reference

THE DARK SIDE OF
GAME TEXTURING

DAVID FRANSON

Premier

Press

INCLUDES CD-ROM

ISBN: 1-59200-350-8
Library of Congress Catalog Card Number: 2004090732
Printed in the United States of America
04 05 06 07 08 BA 10 9 8 7 6 5 4 3 2 1

THOMSON

COURSE TECHNOLOGY

Professional ■ Trade ■ Reference

Course PTR, a division of Course Technology
25 Thomson Place
Boston, MA 02210
http://www.courseptr.com

SVP, Course Professional, Trade, Reference Group:
Andy Shafran

Publisher:
Stacy L. Hiquet

Senior Marketing Manager:
Sarah O'Donnell

Marketing Manager:
Heather Hurley

Manager of Editorial Services:
Heather Talbot

Senior Acquisitions Editor:
Emi Smith

Associate Marketing Manager:
Kristin Eisenzopf

Project/Copy Editor:
Karen A. Gill

Technical Reviewer:
Alex Varanese

Retail Market Coordinator:
Sarah Dubois

Interior Layout Tech:
Susan Honeywell

Cover Designer:
Mike Tanamachi

CD-ROM Producer:
Brandon Penticuff

Indexer:
Kelly Talbot

Proofreader:
Kathy Marshall

For my brother, Andrew.

A meticulous and intelligent individual; also,
our sense of humor only the two of us can understand. I love you, man.

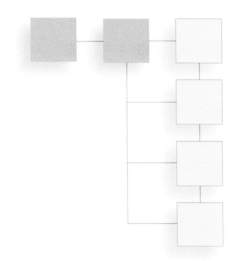

Acknowledgments

Thanks goes out once again to Emi Smith, my acquisitions editor, and to Karen Gill, who was both my project and my copy editor and truly a gem to work with—thank you both, as well as to the rest of the Premier staff! A shot goes out to Alex Varanese, my tech editor, who's a true genius with remarkable programming and graphical talent.

To my mother and father, Shirlee and Bill, for supporting and tolerating me throughout another book. I love you both! To my girlfriend, Michelle, for being so supportive, generous, and understanding of me during the entire length of this book and then some—I love you. To my r/c bud, Mark: During the four months of my writing, we both managed to successfully fly five different planes, as well as successfully crash three against our will—in a single week.

To my black lab, Quilpie, for always being at my side, day and night. Quilpie is the sweetest and most well-behaved dog I've ever seen, and always nuzzling me at my desk while I work.

This is the second book where I've used Photoshop for 2D game content creation; thank you very much Gwyn Weisberg and the rest of the staff at Adobe Systems for such a killer product. Also, my 3D work is as usual generated with Caligari trueSpace and Discreet 3D Studio Max. My hat's off to you all.

Finally, to the awesome game developers iD Software, Gray Matter, and Nerve Software for *Return to Castle Wolfenstein*, which is one of the coolest games out there; to *Valve* and *Gearbox* for *Half-Life*, *Opposing Force*, and the rest of the HL game series; to Epic Games for the *Unreal* series; and to Raven Software for the *Soldier of Fortune*, *Star Trek*, and *Jedi Knight* games. These developers are the most influential to my game graphics creations. Thank you so much.

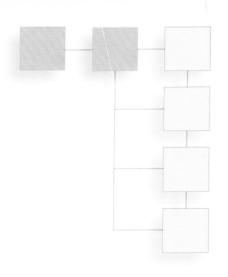

About the Author

David Franson has been a professional in the field of networking, programming, and 2D and 3D computer graphics since 1990. In 2000, he resigned his position as information technology director of one of the largest entertainment law firms in New York City to pursue a full-time career in game development. He is the author of *2D Artwork and 3D Modeling for Game Artists*, as well as the full-page article *How Video Games Are Made*, which appeared in 45 newspapers worldwide. David has also produced digital artwork for 3D video games, film, and television.

Contents at a Glance

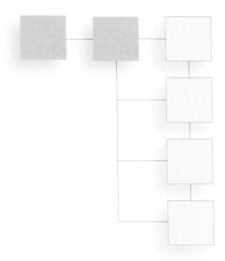

Contents

INTRODUCTION

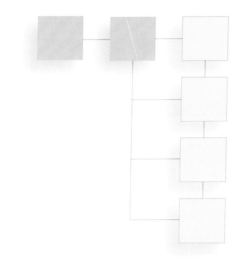

Think sinister alien skin, rotting wood, dripping blood. Imagine twisted metal, dungeon corridors, charred spaceship panels, back alley walls, bullet holes, and blast marks. Wallow in that kind of mire, and you'll appreciate *The Dark Side of Game Texturing*. This book is permeated with dozens of graphics examples dedicated to what I'll call "negative artwork."

If you're like me, you're a big fan of creepy 3D First-Person-Shooter (FPS) games like *Quake, Unreal, Half-Life, Return to Castle Wolfenstein, Max Payne,* and *Undying.* Take a stroll through these games, and you'll see this book smeared over many of the 3D objects, walls, and floors of their levels. It's my intention to analyze the textures in these games, as well as the graphics in some of my favorite movies, and demonstrate how to create many of them, equipped only with a decent PC, Photoshop, and a digital camera.

There are no pretty textures in this book. I think the coolest textures in the world are those found in junkyards, haunted houses, and medieval castles, and I'll bet most serious artists will agree. Movies are great reference points, too. Check out any of the *Alien* series, *Blade Runner, Resident Evil, The Matrix, Saving Private Ryan,* or *Reign of Fire,* and you can easily spot this book (scratched and gouged, edges torn and charred) resting comfortably amidst a heap of rubble. However, I think one of the most important aspects of this book is the fact that if you can create the textures within, you can create *any* texture for *any* game.

What You Need to Know

This book assumes no solid working knowledge of Photoshop. However, this is not a beginning Photoshop book; rather, it's a beginner to intermediate level texturing book. Have no fear; located on this book's CD-ROM is a full Photoshop introduction tutorial in PDF format, written by yours truly. Aren't I nice? If you're completely new to Photoshop or find it difficult to follow along at first, I highly recommend spending a short while familiarizing yourself with the application using my tutorial as a guide. As far as texturing, this book moves fairly quickly. Don't expect the tutorials to be short and snappy; I'll introduce you to basic texturing concepts and Photoshop techniques, and then plunge you straight into the slimy guts of it all!

note

Although this book's tutorials utilize Photoshop version 7, the included latest version on the CD-ROM, Photoshop CS, is nearly identical in layout. Also, almost all the functions and filters packaged with version 6 work as well.

I don't expect you to have a deeply engrained artistic ability. That is, there won't be too much freehand stuff going on here. Rather, I'll be spending more time showing you how to create textures using many of Photoshop's default tools and filters, letting it do much of the work. I do, however, hope that you have a decent working knowledge of the Windows or Macintosh environment, which includes general file manipulation and window handling.

Last, I'm hoping you're an avid 3D video game player. Although many of the texture examples in this book can be used in the 2D/perspective Role-Playing Games (RPGs), I'm leaning more toward those great gory 3D FPS games instead. Those I mentioned earlier aren't *all* hideous through and through; in fact, they can be quite astonishing in visual detail and realism. I always catch myself stopping and staring at empty rooms and their contents and absorbing the artwork. (That is, after I've blown away every ungodly creature in sight.)

What You Need to Have

First and foremost, you must have a computer (d'oh!), either an IBM-compatible or Macintosh. Because you'll need to use Photoshop, Adobe Systems recommends the following for the Windows operating system:

- Intel Pentium III or 4 processor
- Microsoft Windows 98/Me/NT (NT with Service Pack 6a), Windows 2000 with Service Pack 2, or Windows XP

- 128 MB of RAM (192 MB recommended)
- 280 MB of available hard disk space
- 800 × 600 color monitor with 16-bit color or greater video card

And here are the recommendations if you're using a Macintosh:

- PowerPC processor (G3, G4, or G4 dual)
- Mac OS software version 9.1 or 9.2, or Mac OS X version 10.1.3
- 128 MB of RAM (192 MB recommended)
- 320 MB of available hard disk space
- 800 × 600 color monitor with 16-bit color or greater video card

Of course, these are minimum requirements. I *highly* recommend that your computer have the following:

- A large amount of hard disk space (such as 40 GB or more). Photoshop images can get pretty big, and the program itself caches a ton of data there.

- Lots of RAM, hopefully at least 256 MB or more. Photoshop is a bear and fills up memory quick when performing pixel operations like blending and filtering. (When Photoshop runs out of RAM, it reverts to the hard drive, which is much slower.)

- A nice 3D video card, such as an ATI Radeon or nVidia 4/FX. (After all, we're dealing with intensive 3D video games and graphics here, right?)

- A large monitor, 17" or greater, because it makes your life so much easier to see what you're doing!

- A resolution of 1024 × 768 at least. Most graphics professionals use 1280 × 1024 or 1600 × 1200 because it's important to see as much of your art as possible at once.

Besides having a computer, you might find it comes in handy to have a graphics tablet when creating textures for your game environment. Mine is a Wacom 6 × 8 that you can pick up for something like $250 (or even cheaper if you find a used one on http://www.ebay.com). A graphics tablet makes texture creation much, much easier because it's much more like working with pen and paper. These tablets are pressure sensitive, too, which means the amount of pressure you apply with the tablet's digipen dictates the workflow of the tool being used in Photoshop.

Also, a digital camera is invaluable; many textures in games are composites—that is, they are images derived from a photograph combined with artistic effects that you apply. Just make sure your camera, should you purchase one, is capable of at least 2.1-megapixel images, if not more. I have a Kodak DC290 with a maximum 3-megapixel capacity, and I'm considering trading up for something with 5+ megapixel ops.

How This Book Is Organized

This book is straightforward, but I've at least organized the chapters so that they flow together artistically. Chapter 1, "Texturing Basics," introduces you to many of the general concepts you should know about texturing in the gaming world. Texturing isn't just about creating a square image and plopping it into a game. You need to know about pixel sizes, color modes, alpha channels, palettizing, texture sets, image formats, and so on, or the game engine you're using will spit your textures back out at you. This chapter also covers some Photoshop basics that I didn't review in the CD-ROM tutorial that you need to know to handle many of the texturing examples, such as level adjustments, channels and displacement maps, filters, styles, and blending modes.

Chapters 2, "Nasty Decals," through 8, "Sci-Fi Textures," are the meat of the book. They consist of the delicious texturing tutorials that describe the nature inherent in the title of this book. I begin with decals in Chapter 2, which is a nice starting point because it consists of cool rusty signs, bullet holes, blast marks, and anything else that can be quickly tacked onto an existing texture in a game. The rest of the chapters flow with texturing examples such as sprites, military, slums, medieval/fantasy, planetary, and sci-fi.

Finally, the back of the book has three appendixes. Appendix A, "A 2D Graphics Primer," contains an abridged overview of general digital graphics concepts with which you should be familiar. Appendix B, "Photoshop Keyboard Shortcuts," lists all of Photoshop's default keyboard shortcuts. Finally, Appendix C, "Related Web Sites and Links," lists a bunch of great Web sites you might find useful.

What's on the CD-ROM

The CD in the back of the book is crammed with the following:

- Adobe Photoshop CS (version 8) demo for Windows
- Adobe Acrobat Reader for Windows
- A beginner's Photoshop tutorial
- All chapter tutorial files and most of the book's chapter figures
- Hundreds of royalty-free texture images (that is, pictures of things I took for your personal texturing use)

Start Gnashing Your Teeth!

With all of this said, pop your knuckles and get ready to bear down on the tutorials. Toss in your favorite tunes (try Chemical Brothers during the first few chapters) and enjoy these cool texturing tutorials. Have fun with this book and the texture examples herein. Feel free to contact me with any questions or comments at g_lok434@earthlink.net or visit my Web site at http://www.g-lok.com to see the rest of my artwork. Also, notify me or Premier Press if your CD-ROM is invalid in any way. You can reach Premier Press staff through their Web site at http://www.courseptr.com.

Bona fortuna et bene studere!

Good luck and study well!

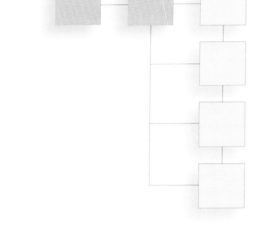

CHAPTER 1

TEXTURING BASICS

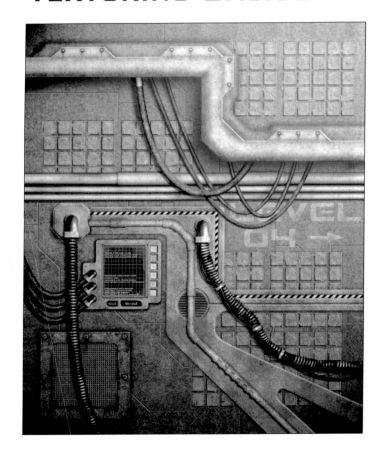

Cum cura docet ut discipuli bene discant…

He teaches with care so that his students may learn well…

Textures are a 2D digital representation of 3D objects. We make a texture to suspend the disbelief that some object in a video game contains detailed, physical geometry, where it doesn't exist. As of the early twenty-first century, texturing for video games and other articles that utilize 3D graphics is important because the computing power at hand doesn't quite allow us to make such highly detailed (high polygon count) 3D objects.

Therefore, a texture is simply a faux finish for a 3D object, like making a wall look like it has pipes and wires running across it. As our computers become more powerful over the next century, we will eventually find that the texture artist will have less work to do and will eventually diminish from his job. We only make textures now to save on processing performance, but after our 3D models contain polygon counts in the millions, we really won't need complex textures. (Of course, this won't be for quite some time!) The models themselves will intrinsically display their own details, and it will just be a matter of coloring a 3D object's individual vertices.

In this chapter, you will learn the following:

- What the most common game textures are and how they're used
- What creating base textures entails, and what their general composition is
- The general Photoshop techniques used in creating textures in this book
- How to create textures with proper file parameters in Photoshop
- How to set up your finished textures for various game engines
- How to preview your textures in games
- Some all-around advice when creating and using different types of textures

Types of Textures

In the real world of Pentium 4 computers and the like, textures are still a critical component of 3D models. Your ability to create great realism in your textures that mimics the real thing is key. Textures also vary in type. Some are meant to spread across walls, floors, and landscapes, whereas others are meant to wrap around boulders, machinery, and characters, to name a few. Still others are meant to go on top of existing textures. Let's review some of these types and how they're used, and explore some things to consider when making them.

Seamlessly Tiling Textures

A seamless texture is the most common texture in games because it is used to cover lots of general area, such as walls and grounds. A texture can be seamless in several ways, most commonly being side by side. This means that you can copy and place a seamlessly tileable image next to itself, without a noticeable seam. Most wall textures are of this nature, in that they run in a straight line with a fixed height. (See Figure 1.1.)

Figure 1.1 A seamlessly tileable texture whose left and right sides blend together with copies of itself.

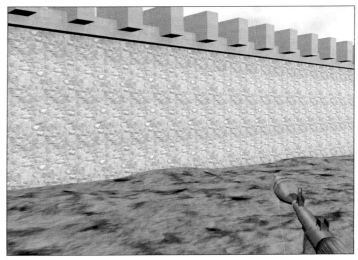

Figure 1.2 A seamless texture that is tileable on all sides. Its internal characteristics show that there's only one texture being used repeatedly on the object.

Textures that are seamless on all sides with copies of itself are generally used for much larger areas that don't run in a straight row, like a large wall or a landscape. However, as you can imagine, a single texture of this nature used on a large surface stands out, should it have any regular characteristics within itself. For instance, in Figure 1.2, I've tiled one such seamless brick texture on a big wall, but you can tell that it's composed of only one texture that's repeated.

To circumvent that noticeable quality of tiling a single texture across vast areas, a texture artist can create what is known as a *randomly tileable texture set*.

Randomly Tileable Sets

Many game engines allow you to create and import a sequence of textures that the game randomly tiles on the wall, floor, or another object of your choice. This can greatly improve on the monotony of a wall that has the same texture tiled all over it, as well as

speed up the process of skinning large walls at the same time.

To create a randomly tileable set of textures (typically somewhere from 4 to 10), each of which is just a bit different but seamlessly blends with any of the others in any direction, is mostly a matter of creating a single texture whose outer edges are seamless when placed next to itself. Then create copies of that texture, and change the copy's innards a bit so that it appears different from the original.

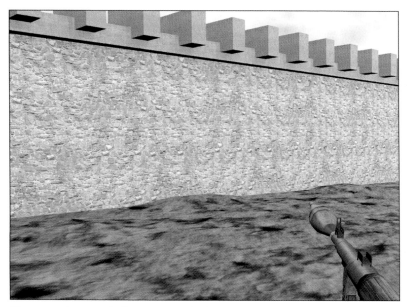

Figure 1.3 Two similar textures tiled on a wall. Not only are the textures seamless with each other, but they also help to break up any noticeable repeating patterns.

Making a randomly tileable set can be easy or difficult, depending on what type of texture you're dealing with. In the case of Figure 1.2, slightly modifying the inner portion of the texture and then saving it as another file name is easy enough. The set could then appear as in Figure 1.3, in which each image is similar to and tileable with the others.

tip

See Chapter 6, "Medieval/Fantasy Textures," for a working example of creating a stone wall texture set that is seamlessly tileable in all directions.

To implement a seamless set in a typical game engine, all you have to do is follow the level editor's proper nomenclature to indicate that it is, in fact, a randomly tileable set. For example, in the case of *Half-Life*, start each texture's name with a - sign, followed by a sequence number starting with 0, and then the name, like so:

-0cementwall.bmp

-1cementwall.bmp

-2cementwall.bmp

-3cementwall.bmp

The editor then takes care of randomly applying these textures to whatever surface you elect. See Chapter 6, where I demonstrate how to create a seamlessly tiling castle wall set.

Here are some things to keep in mind when creating tiling textures:

- Use the Clone Stamp or Healing Brush tool avidly to copy good areas and paste them over bad ones. The Healing Brush tool particularly does a great job with blending cloned areas with the portion on which you're working.

- Use the Clone Stamp tool to even out the texture. Remember to always use a low brush pressure setting in Photoshop when you're using brush tools.

- Dodge shadows and burn highlights out of (or conversely, into) the image. Sometimes shadows and highlights can be a nuisance and strongly stand out in your texture. However, some instances require the addition of shadows and highlights to create the illusion of depth.

- Zoom in on your work to aid in detailed operations.

- Take your time. This is a small piece of work to make a huge wall!

Decals

Decals are small images that are typically coupled with an alpha channel. Decals are placed on top of existing textured objects in a game. If you've ever blown something away that was near a wall, for instance, and seen blood or slime splatter all over the place, or even walked up to a wall and shot it with your AK-47 and created bullet holes, those images are decals overlaid dynamically by the game's engine. A decal can also be a simple metal sign or something that needs to be placed somewhere.

Figure 1.4   ©1998 Epic Games, Inc.
Bullet hole decals applied to a wall in the *Unreal* engine.

The only thing special about these game assets is that they sometimes have transparent sections to them, requiring a single color to represent transparency (an *alpha channel*). The channel that represents transparency is a parameter you need to find out; consult the engine's specifications. For instance, if you're creating a decal for *Half-Life* (using the Worldcraft/Hammer editors), the transparent color is pure white (hex# FFFFFF), whereas a decal in *Unreal* (using UnrealEd) is medium gray (hex# 808080). See Table 1.1 (page 14) for what to think about when you're generating images that have some sort of transparency, particularly for *Return to Castle Wolfenstein 3D*, *Half-Life*, *Unreal*, and the *Torque* engine. Note that levels in *Torque* can also be created using the Worldcraft or Hammer level editor. Figure 1.4 shows a bullet hole decal and its appearance on a wall.

note

Remember that when I refer to a hex#, I'm referring to the hexadecimal number (six alphanumeric characters; three pairs that indicate each RGB channel's brightness value) that represents the exact color in Photoshop's Color Picker. You can change to any color I write about by simply entering this number in the Color Picker's hex# area. See the Photoshop tutorial on the CD-ROM for more detailed information on this.

The only other thing you should keep in mind when creating this stuff is what will be the base material to which the decals are applied. You'll be doing bullet holes in the next chapter, but not every hole will look good on every surface. Therefore, it might be necessary to make an arsenal of bullet-hole decals that you can put on a wide range of objects.

Alpha Transparency-Based Textures

In most 3D games, there are times when an object (or *brush*, in level-design lingo) is present that the player must be able to see through, such as a catwalk, ladder, or chain-link fence. Instead of making a high-poly mesh

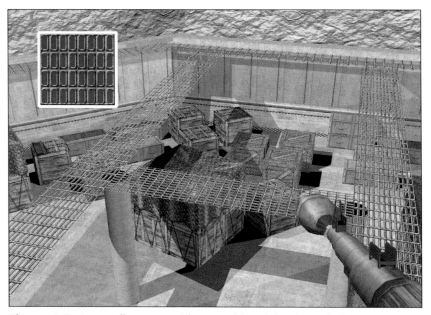

Figure 1.5 A catwalk texture with a pure blue alpha channel. The game engine renders everything except the pure blue portions, making the texture see-through.

model, you can simply create a texture with an alpha channel as its see-through portion. The game's engine interprets a predefined alpha channel, or single color (typically either pure blue, black, or gray) as the color that won't be rendered.

Figure 1.5 shows a tileable catwalk texture that is placed on a plane brush that you could use in *Half-Life*. *Half Life*'s engine renders all shades of blue

except pure blue (hex# 0000FF); therefore, it only displays the catwalk portion of the texture. This opens the door for a wide variety of tricks to simulate normally difficult-to-model items. For instance, if you've played *Return to Castle Wolfenstein*, you've occasionally seen cobwebs swaying in a breeze in the catacombs. This is simply some lightly brushed, grayish-white color on a black background, and the texture is placed on a single plane object and placed into position.

As you can imagine, you can simulate quite a plethora of things in video games by using alpha channeled textures, from blood splat decals, to windows, animated smoke sprites, and fires to name a few. Again, Table 1.1 lists common alpha colors used in popular game engines. All you have to do is consult the documentation for the engine you're using to obtain these color predefinitions.

U-V Based Textures

A texture for a 3D object (called a *skin*) is based on what is called a U-V map. For instance, when I model a weapons crate in a 3D program like 3D Studio Max (not a major chore; it's just a cube), the object is composed of visible vertices, interconnected with edges, that define its overall shape. Directly associated with these vertices are *U-V coordinates*, which are merely invisible copies of each of the vertices. Both are initially located in each other's same position. These coordinates define how the object's texture wraps itself around it. U and V (and sometimes W) are simply the X, Y,

and Z Cartesian coordinates of the 3D object. We use the letters U and V when speaking about the texture coordinates, however.

Most 3D programs have a separate portion dedicated to manipulating the U-V coordinates of an object so that you can create a U-V texture map, making it much easier to create and wrap a good texture around it. Other programs like Right Hemisphere's DeepUV are dedicated to quickly and easily "unwrapping" the U-V coordinates and laying them out flat on a 2D texture map. In Figure 1.6, I've used this program to unwrap the U-V coordinates of a cube, lay them flat, and then use Photoshop to create a texture for it.

If you want some really cool, good U-V tutorials using 3D Studio Max and DeepUV, check out my book titled *2D Artwork and 3D Modeling for Game Artists*. There, I detail the U-V unwrapping and skinning process for both a weapon and a character model. See Chapter 4, "Military Textures," where I demonstrate a cool weapon skin. The unwrapping process isn't explained, however; that's subject matter for a 3D modeling book like the one I just mentioned!

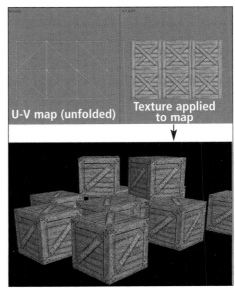

Figure 1.6
The U-V texture coordinates of a cube, unwrapped and laid out flat on a texture map. When a texture is painted in Photoshop using this map as a reference, the texture wraps around the cube effortlessly.

Bump and Displacement Maps

Bump maps and displacement maps are similar in that they are grayscale images that are used as height maps for textures or 3D models. A bump map is used in conjunction with a texture to simulate 3D surfaces on a

3D object. This generally reduces the polygon count of an object; instead of meshing out, say, a bumpy dinosaur skin by creating a 20,000 polygon model, you can use a bump map and a 2,000 polygon count model. The bump map is a grayscale map that the game or modeling engine uses to shade the existing texture. The engine interprets the varying shades of gray as white is highest, black is lowest.

You can also use Photoshop to render a Lighting Effect filter using a bump map; I demonstrate this several times in this book. For instance, the rock texture in Figure 1.7 has a distinct, rough feel to it. I used this filter in conjunction with the associated bump map (also known as a texture channel in Photoshop) shown to obtain this rendering.

A displacement map, on the other hand, is a black-and-white texture that is commonly used by a 3D modeling program or game engine to generate a game's terrain. The software interprets the varying shades of gray in the map as different height values for the terrain, and based on that

information generates a 3D mesh object that becomes the actual surface on which players move around. This is a far more efficient way to create realistic and random terrains, rather than by modeling them by hand. Bryce 3D is also a great program that can not only assist in creating terrain displacement maps, but also generate 3D terrain models. Figure 1.8 shows a terrain displacement map used to create a landscape in the *Torque* game engine.

Animated Textures

As computers become more powerful, you'll see animated textures diminish and be replaced by particle systems. However, it takes a lot of processing power to render hundreds of thousands of tiny polygons flowing or bouncing

Figure 1.7
A bump map is used in Photoshop to render a rough-looking rock texture.

Figure 1.8 GarageGames, ©2000–2004
A displacement map can also be used to auto-generate a complex terrain, instead of having to model it by hand.

all over the place, as in billowing smoke or a shower of sparks. As a substitute, you can create an animation sequence, also known as a *sprite* (usually by rendering it out in a special sprite animation program or even 3D Studio Max), and render the animation frame-by-frame to individual image files. Then it's just a matter of properly naming the files according to the game engine of choice. For instance, in the *Unreal* engine, each file in an animation sequence is named as NAME_A#.PCX, where # begins with 00. An explosion animation sequence would be named something like this:

explode_A00.pcx

explode_A01.pcx

explode_A03.pcx, and so on

Figure 1.9 shows one of the explosion animation sequences found in *Unreal Tournament*. Notice that pure black (hex#000000) is the color used as the alpha channel, which won't be rendered. After the animation is imported into the engine, it's a matter of placing it on a plane in the *Unreal* Editor and setting the animation's parameters, such as

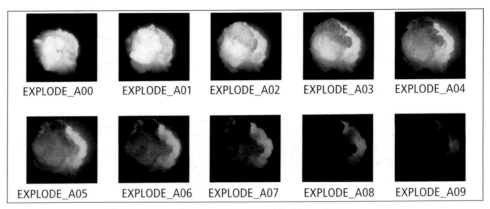

EXPLODE_A00	EXPLODE_A01	EXPLODE_A02	EXPLODE_A03	EXPLODE_A04
EXPLODE_A05	EXPLODE_A06	EXPLODE_A07	EXPLODE_A08	EXPLODE_A09

Figure 1.9 An explosion animation sequence used in *Unreal Tournament*.

frame rate, repetition, and so on.

Other forms of animated textures can be blinking lights on a control panel, running water, phaser blasts, electrical arcs, and moving clouds to name a few. Also, fire and smoke sprite animations often are placed on multiple, crossed planes to give them a volumetric look. Figure 1.10 shows one such grouping of fire texture animations in *Return to Castle Wolfenstein*. Note that this game was built using the *Quake 3 Arena* game engine.

Figure 1.10 ©2002 Id Software, Inc.
Some animations, as in this fire in *Return to Castle Wolfenstein*, consist of several sequences placed on different, crossed planes to produce a volumetric look.

Base Texture Images

Nearly all the texture examples in this book begin their life with the creation of a root, or base texture. Most of the time, I elect to use one or several photographs of something that already contains a texture that is suitable for the overall texture I'm creating, such as the side of a rusty dumpster, a brick wall, or a wood plank. Trying to reproduce these base images from scratch in Photoshop is far too painful and time consuming because a real-world texture photograph is usually a complex mix of elements. Therefore, the best thing you can do is plan out your texture by deciding what it will consist of, and then whip out your trusty digital camera and head out.

A great example is the texture you saw at the beginning of this chapter. My girlfriend happened to have this nasty, rusty piece of metal paneling hidden behind her backyard shed, and to my delight she let me keep it! I'm not quite sure why she wanted to part with it or where she got it in the first place. In Figure 1.11, I took a picture of the panel up close, and took samples from it to create not only the base texture in

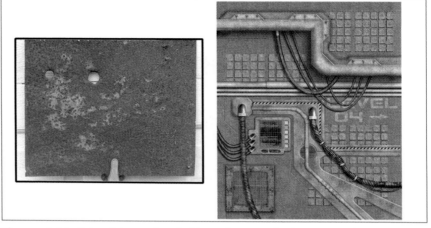

Figure 1.11 Take pictures of real objects that contain the texture elements you need when creating a texture. The digital photograph here was used to create nearly every element in the final texture.

the image, but also color variations of it to generate most of the pipe work and other details. See Chapter 8, "Sci-Fi Textures," where I create more textures like this based on these types of photographs.

tip

It's good to know the makeup of real-world materials when you're building your textures. For example, when making formed cement walls, engineers don't just take a batch of plain, smooth cement and pour it into a form to make the wall block. If they did, the mildest of vibrations or pressure over time would cause the cement to become unstable and break apart. Instead, engineers mix the cement with cracked stones and put a thick grid of ribbed steel rods, called *rebar* (reinforcement bar), into the center of the cement formers. That means that if you decide to make a cement wall that has been blasted away in one area by, say, a 50 mm shell, you'll want keep in mind that in the real world, cement walls contain stone and rebar, and render them accordingly.

You should be aware of several issues when snapping pictures of things outside. First, be sure to have a camera that is capable of taking pictures with at least a 3-megapixel resolution. The average camera out there (as of late 2003) has about a 5.1 megapixel capacity, which is more than ample for texturing work. The picture in Figure 1.11 was taken with a Kodak DC290, which uncompressed was about 3.1 megapixel, and worked just fine.

Lighting is the second key. There's no better substitute for lighting than our own sun because it contains the full spectrum of visible light and reflects the maximum amount of color information from objects you're photographing. It's best to get your images with the sun at the low horizon, usually in the morning (this will vary depending on your latitude). The one thing you need to watch out for, however, is highlights and shadows. When the sun is high overhead, it creates reflective hot spots and harsh shadows. A picture of, say, a brick wall in this mode makes it much more difficult to extrapolate a base texture or seamless textures from it. (See Figure 1.12.) If you were to drop the brick texture on the left into a game engine

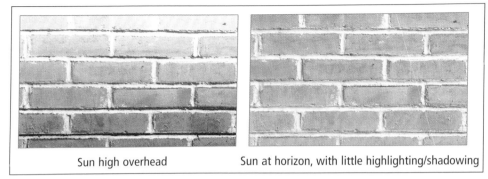

Sun high overhead | Sun at horizon, with little highlighting/shadowing

Figure 1.12 Highlights and shadows from the sun or another lighting source can ruin a base texture. This makes it much more difficult to extrapolate base or seamless textures from it.

whose lighting wasn't coming from above, it would look out of place.

As a rule of thumb, try to get a picture of your object when the sun is hitting it straight on (perpendicular to).

Finding Texture Images

Unless you live in a desert (no offense to any desert-ians—I was born in a desert in California) you'll find that you won't have to travel far to get good base texture pictures. If you're fortunate to live close to a big city, you can probably find just about every texture you'll ever need. I live right near New York City, and a while ago I took hundreds of photos all over the place; those images are included with

this book's CD-ROM and are yours to use royalty free. How nice of me! Anyway, just be careful when taking pictures in a big city—since the 9/11 attacks, people are weary about photographers, and in some cases you could get your camera confiscated. That almost happened to me twice, once in New York and once when I was just taking pictures of the side of a mall in my home town! The following is a great list of other places to find outstanding and unique textures:

- Junkyards
- Old rotting barns
- Industrial plants (be sure to get permission first)

- Warehouses
- 200+ year-old buildings and houses, or even better, a castle
- Churches and synagogues

Texture File Creation in Photoshop

Depending on the game engine used, most textures have a fixed size, resolution, and file type. (See Table 1.1.) However, most textures begin with a large size and resolution so that you can create small details with ease; then, when the texture is complete, you resize for the engine (typically either 512 × 512 or 256 × 256 pixels). The dimensions of the textures are always divisible by either 8 or 16; many game engines require this.

In this book, I generally start with a large square texture base like 1024 × 1024 or 2048 × 2048 pixels, with a 2048-Dot-Per-Inch (DPI) resolution. (See Figure 1.13.) This provides more than an ample amount of potential detail. You really only need the DPI at around 300, but I keep it the same as the dimensions so that when I resize the DPI to, say, 256, the image's dimensions move to 256 × 256 as well, making the overall image a

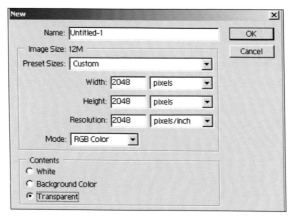

Figure 1.13 Typical new texture file setup in this book.

one-square-inch print. As you'll see in the chapters that follow, with these high resolutions, you can zoom in and create minute elements, which are typical of print production work.

Notice that I begin with a transparent background in a new image; if you start with a white background, an unlockable Background layer is created. A transparent background simply starts off with Layer 1 as the background, allowing you to jockey it around with other layers.

Notice also that the color mode of the new file is RGB. In Appendix A, "A 2D Graphics Primer," I discuss color modes and channels, so it would be a good idea to quickly review those to get a decent understanding of them. RGB is necessary to gain the full potential of Photoshop; many of the filters are disabled when in other modes, so create everything in RGB, and then convert to other formats at the end.

Cover Art

Cover art for print has file parameters that are a bit different from game textures. Most people don't take full advantage of their own home color printer's capabilities. Generally speaking, creating cover art quality such as that printed in books and magazines requires the final image to be quite huge, in the neighborhood of 7.375" × 9.125" at 300 DPI. Try creating that in Photoshop; you'll see that the base, blank image with no elements already takes up 17.3 MB of memory! Finally, when you're done with your image, including layers and whatnot, you'll find you can easily generate a 100-MB file. But that is because the image is now matching a printer's abilities. Try creating an image like this and print it on glossy photo paper, and you'll get professional, magazine-quality prints.

Creating Textures in Photoshop

Before I thrust you into any cool texturing tutorials, I'm going to assume you have at least a fundamental knowledge of Photoshop—that is, you know how to create and save images, use the toolbar and its tools, make selections, and manage layers. If not, and you're completely new to Photoshop, have no fear! Look to the Photoshop tutorial located on the CD-ROM; there you'll find a concise and comprehensive review of everything you need to know—at least, up to here.

Most of what I teach in this book deals with the intermediate and (fairly infrequent) advanced use of Photoshop. For instance, you'll need a firm grasp of layers and channels; most beginners find layers and channels somewhat confusing, but they're a priceless commodity, I guarantee it. If you are a Photoshop beginner, review Appendix A for all of the color mode and pixel basics you should know. Finally, it will truly help your texturing efficiency by using a good dozen of Photoshop's

keyboard shortcuts; see Appendix B, "Photoshop Keyboard Shortcuts," for a complete listing. You don't need to know all the shortcuts, but at least review the first set I list there, which are those I use the most.

After the base image is in place in your texture, the next process is filling in the image. This book covers a wide variety of texturing techniques, most of which are operations that Photoshop has to offer. Usually, these techniques are creating what appear to be 3D elements but are simulated by use of styles and filters. I constantly use styles to create bevels and drop shadows, and filters for adding an almost tangible texture feel to the image. There's little in the way of hand-painted art here. I don't consider myself a classic artist in any way, and I can't assume you are either. Instead, the textures rely mostly on the careful use of many of Photoshop's built-in functions.

Using 3D Models

There are, however, certain times when it is difficult to create a 3D element in an image solely by using Photoshop's tools. If you have access to a 3D modeling program like trueSpace or a

freeware one like Milkshape 3D, it's much easier to just create a 3D model and render it to file, and then insert it into your texture. The image in Figure 1.11 shows a couple of greenish, bellowed hoses hanging straight down; these I created and rendered in trueSpace, and then blended them right in with the rest of the image. I demonstrate this technique later on in Chapter 8, as well as provide you with the 3D file and prerendered image of it.

Setting Up Textures for a Game

I'd like to give you a heads up on how you might prepare your textures for whatever game engine you're working with. I said earlier that your textures should be evenly divisible by some multiple of 8 or 16. This is a good rule to follow for several reasons. For one, game engines are coded following certain rules spawned by the language by which they are generated. The language (most probably C++) works with variables to store numbers that are powers of two (binary); typically, these variables are 8 and 16 bit. Therefore, you want your engine to deal with external assets, such as textures, that have dimensions that are at least divisible by two or by a factor of two, such as 16.

Another reason to keep your textures dimensionally consistent is for placing them in the level you're designing. It would be cumbersome to have to constantly tweak and adjust textures for walls and other objects if the textures had all sorts of weird measurements. It would be much better if, for instance, your wall textures were all 256 × 256 pixels in size. Then all you would have to do is create walls that were 256 pixels high, make your editing environment snap to multiples of 16, and easily place the texture map(s) on the walls.

Finally, in many cases, game engines require that your bitmap be constrained within a maximum size and that it also be divisible by some binary multiple. For instance, if you are developing textures for *Half-Life*, your texture bitmaps are limited to a maximum size of 256 × 256 pixels, must be 8-bit BMPs, and the length and width must be divisible by 2. On the other hand, the *Unreal* engine's ceiling allows for a maximum size of 1024 × 1024 pixels (although you'll find that most of the textures in *Unreal* are not much bigger than 256 × 256), either the length or the width must be divisible by 2, and the images must be either 8-bit PCXs or BMPs. Newer engines and newer graphics cards allow for higher-resolution textures, but a 1024 × 1024-pixel image is as much eye candy as I want to ingest! See Table 1.1 for a listing of several game engines and their texture requirements.

Table 1.1 Typical Game Engine Texture Specifications

Game/Engine	Texture File Type	Max File Size	Level Editor Used	Editor Download Location	General Brush Transparency	Decal Transparency	Sprite Transparency
Quake 3 Arena	JPG/TGA	1024 × 1024	Q3Radiant	http://www.quake3world.com	Black, located in 32-bit TGA alpha channel	Black	Black
Half-Life	BMP	256 × 256 pixel	Worldcraft/ Hammer	http://collective.valve-erc.com	Blue (hex# 0000FF)	White (hex# FFFFFF)	Black (grayscale variable, where hex# 000000 is 100% transparent)
Unreal	PCX, BMP	1024 × 1024 pixel	UnrealEd	n/a	Black (grayscale variable)	Gray (hex# 808080)	Black
Torque	PNG, JPG	512 × 512 pixel	Worldcraft/ Hammer/Press F11 for Terrain Editor	http://collective.valve-erc.com	None (uses Photoshop's transparency in PNG format)		

Note: See Appendix A for more information on file types.

Resize and Palettize

If you've played any 3D first-person game since the turn of the new millennium, the walls that constitute the boundaries of your environment were probably adorned with 256 × 256-pixel textures either seamlessly tiled using just one image or using a tileable set. From analyzing these games, I've noticed that the lead character's height is typically in the ballpark of 128 to 177 pixels, or just over half the height of a texture panel (in level-editor measurements, this generally translates to a character height of around two meters). As an example, when you're finished creating your texture in Photoshop and want to prepare your texture for *Unreal*, choose Image, Image Size, and set the dimensions to 256 × 256. For consistency, you can also set the resolution to 256 pixels per inch, making the overall image size one square inch. (Don't worry about that too much. It only affects the output if you print it.) You might have to uncheck the Constrain Proportions check box to keep the numbers the way you want them. Finally, choose Bilinear resampling, which is a pixel interpolation method that tells Photoshop how to resize the image and how to assign color values to any new pixels it creates, based on the color values of existing pixels in the image. Bicubic is the best method, but it seems to generate a small pixel border around the image and tends to blur the image slightly due to its heavier antialiasing algorithm. I've found that Bilinear is just fine. (See Figure 1.14.)

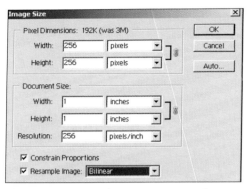

Figure 1.14 Use these parameters when resizing your image in Photoshop; you can use them in most game engines.

The next thing you need to do is palettize the image. You'll be working in RGB (24-bit) color mode, which is typical for any texture creation, but the image will have too much color information for a typical game engine to handle (although some game engines, like the *Torque* engine, will accept it). The programmers of games like *Half-Life* and *Unreal* force artists to *palettize* their textures, or convert their artwork to use a self-contained palette consisting of only 256 (8-bit) colors. This will help to dramatically speed up the game without much loss of texture quality (sort of).

To palettize your image, click Image, Mode, Indexed Color. Set your palette to Local (Selective) and Colors to 256. This makes Photoshop analyze your image and select the best matching 256 colors to stick in an accompanying palette, which is subsequently stored in the BMP or PCX file when you save the texture. Also, set Forced to None. Later on, you can do something advanced like force your texture groups to use a common palette for game optimization. When everything is set, click OK. Now your image has only 256 colors, and it's ready to be saved as a BMP or PCX file. (See

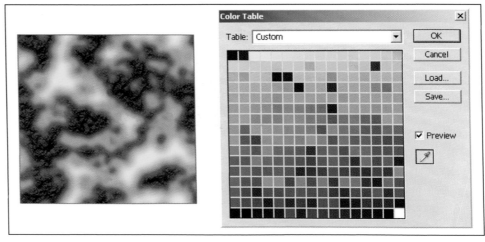

Figure 1.15 A texture resized for a 3D game engine. Note the color table (palette) that the image uses.

Figure 1.15.) You can see the actual palette your file will use by clicking Image, Mode, Color Table.

Creating a Set That Shares the Same Palette

Let's assume you've created a number of similar textures that will be part of a set. For instance, say that you have a spaceship deck, or many decks, that have those caution lines tracing all over the place. Maybe they're a path for a robot or something. It might be a good idea to make a nice set of textures that can be flipped and arranged to create any number of caution-line patterns.

When you create each texture, reduce the image, and then palettize the image for final import into a game, you might want to force these textures to share the same color palette—after all, how much different are the colors between each texture? If tiles share the same palette, the game's engine can load a single palette (hence making the game run faster).

To see what I mean, from the previous example, palettize your image. (Click Image, Mode, Indexed Color.) Set the Colors to 256, and then pull down the Palette list and select Custom. You'll then get a Color Table dialog box.

Finally, click the Save button to save this palette. (Pick whatever file name you want.)

The next time you create another similar texture and change the mode to Indexed Color, just click Custom Palette again and load the palette you saved. The textures will share the same palette without loss of color data, and the game will be optimized.

Viewing Your Textures

You can apply and view your textures in 3D games simply by using the particular game's *level editor*. Some games come with their own editor, such as *Unreal*'s UnrealEd, whereas others like *Half-Life* require the Hammer editor, which you can download for free from Valve-ERC at http://collective.valve-erc.com/. The editor's documentation will describe how to import and apply your textures to brush objects. UnrealEd is particularly easy to use, so it's good for previewing your work.

A completed 256 × 256-pixel texture might look small and silly, but after it's brought into a game, it regains its proportions. In Figure 1.16, I took a

Figure 1.16 Importing and applying the finalized brick texture into a game engine.

256 × 256 brick texture and made a simple street corner in a game. It could use a bit of finesse, but it will work, don't you think?

Another way to preview your work is in a 3D modeling program such as 3D Studio Max or trueSpace. For instance, within those programs, you can create a cube or 2-meter high wall and paint your texture on it. To mimic a common game engine's rendering resolution, set the texture rendering parameters to 256 or 512 pixels.

Final Advice on Texture Creation

Texture creation is not a random process. A good artist spends time creating and organizing textures to fit a particular scene or level so that everything comes together somewhat fluently, and that nothing seems out of place. Textures are usually created in sets; that is, if you're creating a dungeon, you'll create a "dungeon set" by grouping appropriate artwork for the stone walls, floors, and ceilings. You'll create wood textures for the doors, stretching racks, torches, and the like.

Here's a quick guideline/overview of what you should think about before embarking on texture-creation projects:

- The more time you spend on a texture, the better (or more realistic) it will look. On the other hand, as with any business, time is money. Work fast, but work well.

- There's more than one way to skin a cat. Always think of the fastest or best way to perform any particular step while creating your textures. No one way is the absolute correct way!

- Work large and reduce. Don't try to create a tileable stone wall that starts off the size of your thumb. By putting in details on a large image and then reducing the whole thing, you'll get how-did-you-do-that results.

- Understand everything that each room or scene is trying to convey. Is it happy or sad? What decade or era is it set in? Have detailed knowledge of what your game company wants, and then research the materials you'll be creating before you begin. If you're not sure, don't just try to come up with a texture in your head. Use life as your reference! Break out your camera and go to town. Literally.

- Group and work with textures in sets. Don't work randomly.

- Don't make a texture stand out unless it needs to. Blend it nicely with its surroundings.

- Be patient. A game's graphics content can make it sell.

- Don't reinvent the wheel. If a texture exists in some picture, use that instead of re-creating it from scratch.

- Don't be too detailed unless the game's engine calls for it. In fact, the average game's texture is around 256 × 256 pixels in size; not a whole lot of detail can be crammed into that.

Summary

Textures are a 2D bitmap representation of 3D objects. We create textures as a faux finish for 3D objects not only to reduce the overall polygon count of them, thereby increasing the processing performance of a computer, but also to add greater realism to a 3D environment. As you have seen, different types of textures vary depending on the surface of the model in question, from tileable textures for walls and floors, to decals, U-V maps, displacement maps, and animated textures. Some textures are even coupled with a transparency color for use in special situations where they need to be see-through.

Creating textures is not a simple process; careful planning and preparation must be made, especially when designing them for a particular game engine. In this chapter, I reviewed not only the techniques used to create base textures and their internal details, but also how to prepare textures for a variety of game engines. Each game engine that exists on the market can demand its own texture parameters, such as file size and format, file naming conventions, transparency colors, and prepalettizing, to name a few. I provided you with this information here to prepare you for the great texturing chapters that follow so that you can have the knowledge of how to properly use your textures in a gaming environment.

CHAPTER 2

NASTY DECALS

Audaces fortuna iuvat…

Fortune favors the bold…

As I discussed in Chapter 1, "Texturing Basics," decals are special textures that usually contain an alpha channel (special color interpreted by a game engine as transparent). These textures are overlaid on existing textures in a game. Decals can be static or dynamic; that is, as a level designer, you could place a sign decal on a wall that already has a tiled texture, or the game engine can call a bullet hole texture and instantly slap it on that same wall as a game character shoots it. Sprayed logos and blood splats are other examples of dynamically applied decals. It's up to you, however, to determine the decal parameters required by the game engine you're using. Typically, you can find this by downloading and reading the game engine's level editor or Software Development Kit (SDK).

In this chapter, I will show you how to create the following:

- A variety of decals that you can use in any game engine, with specific examples of setting them up in *Return to Castle Wolfenstein*

- Blast marks, bullet holes, and blood splats
- Pipes, rivets, and screws
- Peeling paint on metal
- Dripping effects
- Metal and wooden sign decals

If you haven't read Chapter 1, you're missing out on some essential decal details such as alpha channel transparency concepts and game engine decal parameters. Check out that chapter before trying these tutorials so you can get a handle on the steps I'm taking to make the images here!

tip

If you own *Quake III*, *Return to Castle Wolfenstein*, or any other game that uses the *Quake III* engine, you can view and modify the game's textures (including decals and sprites), as well as the models and maps. Just use PakScape (downloadable from http://www.fileplanet.com), Game File Explorer, or WinZip. WinZip only unzips the PK3 files, and it's a more difficult route in which to add your own textures to aPK3 package. See Chapter 3, "Sprites," for an example of how I alter some of the sprite animations in *Return to Castle Wolfenstein*.

tip

You can download the GtkRadient level editor for *Return to Castle Wolfenstein* if you want to edit levels and add your decals and textures to the game. (Go to http://www.qeradiant.com.) Also, you can download Valve's Hammer editor and SDK to do the same in *Half-Life*. Just go to http://www.valve-erc.com. The SDK also contains good documentation for creating textures that are meant specifically for *Half-Life*. Obviously, you have to purchase a copy of the games first.

File Setup for Decals

Despite the fact that I'm going to set up and demonstrate the images in this chapter specifically for *Return to Castle Wolfenstein*, you can easily change the tutorials a bit for other game engines simply by altering the transparency color value for the decal. (See Table 1.1 in Chapter 1 for a sample of typical decal parameters.) This game, however, uses the *Quake III* engine; therefore, sometimes it requires you to put the transparency information in a separate color channel within a TGA file; other times, it's simply pure black in the image that indicates the transparent regions.

Decals in this game engine (as well as most others) vary in size, but they are usually powers of 2. Keeping texture sizes like this not only helps the programmers when they write the game code, but it makes it easier to architect the game environment by having general buildings and static objects snap to increments of 16 (by which all powers of 2 are evenly divisible). Some common sizes for sign decals, for instance, are 128 × 64 pixels; 64 × 64 for a blood splat or bullet hole; and so on. Still, the key here is to work large and then reduce. If it's a blood splat, start off your image at 512 × 512 pixels, and when finished, in Photoshop click Image, Image Size, and change the width and height to 64 × 64.

Finally, it's a good idea to create the image with a transparent background. That is, when clicking File, New, check Transparent in the Contents section. Then, before you create the alpha (transparency) channel for the image, save your file as a Photoshop PSD file. That way, you can always come back to the file and easily change the alpha channel/transparency color for other game engines.

Blast Marks

In *Return to Castle Wolfenstein* (from now on, I'm going to call it *Wolfenstein*), you'll often see a residual decal of a blast mark on a wall that was hit by something like the Panzerfaust, or rocket-propelled grenade launcher. Typically, blast marks are just smoky, blotchy/radial marks of varying transparency that are applied immediately after the weapon's strike. In Figure 2.1, you can see a Panzerfaust blast mark from *Wolfenstein*.

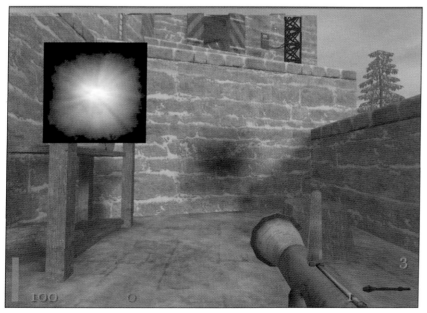

Figure 2.1   ©2002 Id Software, Inc.
A residual blast mark decal left from the Panzerfaust bazooka in *Return to Castle Wolfenstein* (decal inset in the upper-left corner).

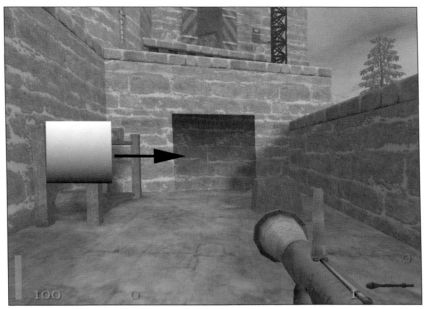

Figure 2.2   © 2002 Id Software, Inc.
Decal transparencies in JPG format act in gradient fashion in *Return to Castle Wolfenstein*. The more black that's in the image, the more transparent it becomes.

As you can see, this decal utilizes a different form of transparency, according to its game engine rules. Decals of this nature in JPG form are in RGB format but are also grayscale. That is, as the colors in the image gradient from 100 percent white to 100 percent black, the engine displays only the white information as black, and then fades off to completely transparent as the white fades to black. It's easier to see this in Figure 2.2. I replaced the Panzerfaust decal with a grayscale gradient; here you can see how this gradient transparency works.

Note also that the game engine randomly rotates the decal to create some variance; this is typical of bullet holes and sprite animations as well. Decals in *Wolfenstein* can either be a TGA with an alpha channel, or simply a JPG with black as the 100 percent transparent color. See the "Bullet Holes" section for an example of using this TGA/alpha channel combination.

Instead of a creating a blotchy decal like in Figure 2.1, I'd rather see one with more of a radial spray mark. So here we go...

1. In Photoshop, start a new 512 × 512-pixel RGB image with a transparent background layer.

2. Fill the image with pure white (hex# FFFFFF).

3. Start a new layer.

4. Select the Airbrush tool. For the tool's Brush type, choose a pixelated, radial pattern, such as Spatter 59 Pixels. (If that's not on the Brush type list, you need to add brushes to your list under Edit, Preset Manager.)

tip

Remember: When I speak of hex#s, I'm referring to the hexadecimal value you can manually enter into Photoshop's Color Picker to get the exact color of which I'm speaking.

5. Press D to reset the Color Picker so that the foreground color is pure black. Spray a black spot directly in the center of the new layer. Use the guides or grid to align the spot. (See Figure 2.3.)

Figure 2.3
Spray a small blotchy pattern in the center of the layer.

6. With this top layer still active, choose Edit, Transform, Scale. Scale up the pattern equally until it covers about 70 percent of the image. (See Figure 2.4.)

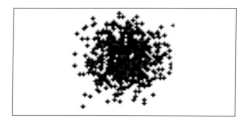

Figure 2.4
Scale up the blotch until it fills a good portion of the image.

7. Choose Filter, Blur, Radial Blur, using the Zoom method. Not too bad for a blast mark, eh? See Figure 2.5.

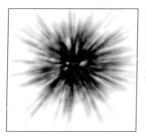

Filter: Blur, Radial Blur
Amount: 100
Blur Method: Zoom
Quality: Good

Figure 2.5
Apply the Radial Blur filter for the final effect.

Figure 2.6
The radial blast mark in action.

To make this decal game-ready for *Wolfenstein*, for example, click Image, Image Size, and change the width and height to 64 pixels. The final image will be thumbnail-sized, but the engine scales it up for you.

Experiment with different base blotch patterns for various blast marks. When you want to see the effect in action, try replacing *Wolfenstein*'s blast mark decal with your own. For this game in particular, you need to navigate to the \MAIN directory and, using a program like Pak-Scape, open the pak0.pk3 file. Then go to the \GFX\ DAMAGE directory and replace the existing burn_med_mrk.jpg file with the new blast mark decal you created. Be sure to use the exact file name, and in JPG format. Then save the PK3 file, and you're ready to go. Figure 2.6 shows my blast mark on a castle wall.

An *Unreal* decal does the same thing, only using medium gray (hex# 808080) as the transparency. Figure 2.7 demonstrates this setup. Remember: It's just a matter of consulting the game engine SDK or level editor's documentation to determine the decal setup parameters.

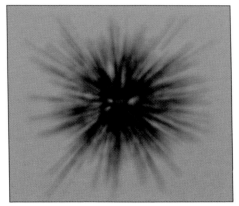

Figure 2.7
The blast mark decal set up for the *Unreal* engine, using pure blue (hex# 808080) as the transparency.

Bullet Holes

Bullet holes can vary from simple to complex; usually they're just a warped black spot over alpha channel transparency. In the examples that follow, I'll again be setting these up for *Wolfenstein*. The difference from the blast mark examples is that these will be 32-bit TGA images with a special alpha channel for transparency.

Bullet Holes on Metal

Most game engines have several bullet hole decals so that they can be applied to objects of varying surface properties, such as metal, wood, and cement. This next example will be a bullet hole meant for metal, with an outward-curving eruption that's typical of metal being torn open.

1. Start a new 512 × 512-pixel RGB image with a transparent background. Fill this background layer with white so that you can see your work.

2. Start a new layer.

3. Press D to reset the swatches.

4. Choose Filter, Render, Clouds.

5. Choose Filter, Render, Difference Clouds. (See Figure 2.8.)

6. Choose Filter, Blur, Gaussian Blur, with a radius of 4.0 pixels.

7. Choose Filter, Sketch, Chrome.

8. Choose Image, Adjust, Levels, and slide the Highlights marker to the left. This gives the texture the appearance of fatigued (or liquid) metal. (See Figure 2.9.)

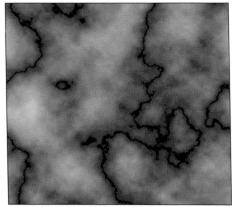

Figure 2.8
Apply the Clouds and then the Difference Clouds filter to a new layer.

Filter: Blur,
Gaussian Blur
Radius: 4.0
pixels
Filter: Sketch,
Chrome
Detail: 10
Smoothness: 0

Figure 2.9
Apply the Gaussian Blur and Chrome filters. Adjust the levels to make the texture look like fatigued steel.

9. With the fatigued-metal layer active, choose Edit, Transform, Scale, and scale down the image evenly about 50 percent. (See Figure 2.10.)

Figure 2.10
Scale down the metal layer 50 percent.

10. Start a new layer.

11. Set your foreground color to black.

12. Using the Airbrush tool (with its brush type set to Soft Round 100 pixels), spray a hole in the middle of the metal. (The paint should be on a separate layer.)

13. Apply an inner bevel to this layer with a medium-gray Highlight Mode color. (See Figure 2.11.)

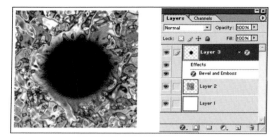

Figure 2.11
Spray a black circle on a new layer, and apply an inner bevel to it.

14. Select the metal layer. (It should be the one between the background and the bullet hole.)

15. Use the Lasso tool to create a jagged selection around the bullet hole. This will be the pattern of the outwardly bent metal. (See Figure 2.12.) In this image, I've enhanced my selection so that it's visible for you in the text.

Figure 2.12
Use the Lasso tool to select a jagged border around the bullet hole.

Style: Bevel and Emboss
Style: Inner Bevel
Technique: Chisel Soft
Depth: 500%
Direction: Down
Size: 10 pixels
Soften: 0
Shading Angle: 90 degrees
Highlight Mode Color: medium-gray, hex# 757373

16. Choose Select, Inverse. You'll be deleting the outside portion of the metal from this selection.

17. Now let's chop up the edges off the selection. First, press Q to enter Quick Mask mode.

18. With the mask active, choose Filter, Brush Strokes, Spatter.

19. Press Q to exit Quick Mask mode.

20. Press Delete to remove the outside metal. (See Figure 2.13.)

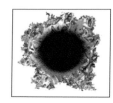

Filter: Brush Strokes, Spatter
Spray Radius: 10
Smoothness: 5

Figure 2.13
Spatter the selection in Quick Mask mode, and then delete the outer portion of the metal.

21. Apply a small drop shadow to the metal layer to give it some height off the surface. It would be better to add shadow evenly all around the metal layer because the *Wolfenstein* engine randomly rotates the decal as it is applied, but for simplicity's sake, I'm leaving it like this.

22. Use the Dodge tool to add highlights around the rim near the hole, and use the Burn tool to darken the edges where the metal appears torn. (See Figure 2.14.) This will make the metal appear to be curving up and down.

Style: Drop Shadow
Blend Mode: Multiply
Opacity: 75
Angle: 90
Distance: 7
Spread: 0
Size: 5

Figure 2.14
Apply a drop shadow to the metal, and then dodge and burn the inside and outside to give it a curved feel.

Okay, that's the completed bullet hole. Now, it's a matter of preparing it for *Wolfenstein* (or whatever engine you choose). For this game, however, the decal needs to have an alpha channel added to the Channels palette to indicate which areas are to be transparent, and which are to be opaque. Follow these steps to complete the decal:

1. Link and merge the top two layers of the bullet hole—that is, just the black spot and the metal layer. Choose Edit, Transform, Scale, and scale the bullet hole up to fill a good 75 percent of the image. Then fill the bottom, background layer with pure black (hex# 000000). (See Figure 2.15.)

Figure 2.15
To prepare the bullet hole decal for *Wolfenstein*, merge the top two layers, scale the bullet hole up about 75 percent, and then fill the bottom layer with pure black.

2. Ctrl+click the top bullet hole layer to load its selection.

3. In the Channels palette, click the Create New Channel button to start a new alpha channel.

4. With the selection still active, press Alt+Backspace to fill the selection with white. The white areas of the alpha channel represent the opacity of the decal, whereas the black areas represent the transparency. (See Figure 2.16.) The game engine will look at this channel to determine what portions of the decal to draw, and what not to draw.

5. Flatten the image by clicking Layer, Flatten Image. Click Image, Image Size, and change the width and height to 64 pixels. Now save the image as a 32-bit TGA file, and it's ready to go. Note that you must save it as 32 bit; this represents a 24-bit color image with the extra 8-bit alpha channel for transparency information.

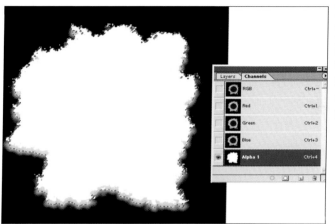

Figure 2.16
Load the bullet hole selection and fill it with white in a new channel. The black in the alpha channel will represent the transparent areas in *Wolfenstein*.

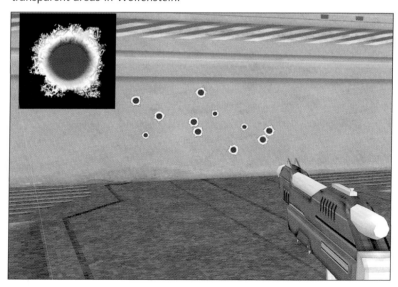

Figure 2.17
The bullet hole decal saved as a TGA file with an alpha transparency channel, ready for a *Quake III* engine.

Now that the decal is of proper size, has a transparency alpha channel, and is a TGA, it is ready for the *Wolfenstein* (or *Quake III*) engine. (See Figure 2.17.)

Note that not only do the many 3D game engines randomly rotate the decals, but they also randomly size the decals.

tip

Group a cluster of different-sized bullet holes onto a decal for shotgun effects. Dust the areas between the holes using a black airbrush to simulate the blast powder.

Bullet Holes on Cement

When a projectile hits something like cement, stucco, mortar, tiles, or whatever, it doesn't just leave a clean hole like it might on metal. Instead, the substance appears to crumble in a cone-shaped pattern that has several layers.

1. Open the cementwall.jpg file from the Chapter 2 section on the CD-ROM. This is a 512 × 512-pixel RGB image cropped from a picture I took of a classic cement/stucco wall from a restaurant a few blocks away from the Game Developers Conference in San Jose.

2. Use the Lasso tool to create a misshapen circle that takes up a good portion of the image.

(See Figure 2.18.) This will be the outer shape of the erosion.

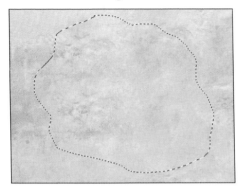

Figure 2.18
Create a circular selection with the Lasso tool.

tip

I highly recommend that you record this as an action at this point because you'll want to make several variants of the same technique.

3. Press Q to enter Quick Mask mode.

4. Apply the Spatter Filter to the selection to chop up the edges.

5. Press Q again to exit the mode.

6. Right-click on the selection and choose Layer Via Copy. This will separate the selection onto its own layer, preserving the background layer.

7. Apply an inner bevel to this new layer to recess the cement. (See Figure 2.19.)

Figure 2.19
Spatter the edges of the selection, copy the selection to a new layer, and apply an inner bevel to recess it.

Filter: Brush Strokes, Spatter
Spray Radius: 15
Smoothness: 5
Style: Bevel and Emboss
Style: Inner Bevel
Technique: Chisel Hard
Depth: 200%
Direction: Down
Size: 10 pixels
Soften: 0
Shading Angle: 90 degrees

8. Ctrl+click this layer to reload the selection.

9. Choose Select, Modify, Contract, and enter a value of 15 pixels. This will reduce the selection.

10. Repeat steps 3–9 several times until you have several layers, creating a cone- or bowl-shaped erosion mark. (See Figure 2.20.)

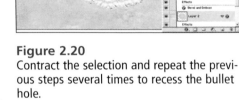

Figure 2.20
Contract the selection and repeat the previous steps several times to recess the bullet hole.

11. Ctrl+click the smallest layer to load the selection, and then fill it with black.

12. Choose Filter, Blur, Gaussian Blur, with a radius of 1.0 pixel, to complete the effect. (See Figure 2.21.) You can now link the erosion layers (except for the background layer), merge them, and scale the bullet hole to size, at 64 × 64 pixels.

Now you can fill the background layer with black, create an alpha channel, and save the decal as a 32-bit TGA file, as I showed you in the previous example. Check out Figure 2.22; here, I've combined the blast mark and bullet-hole techniques onto a single texture,

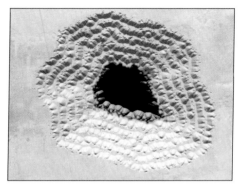

Figure 2.21
Fill the smallest erosion layer with black, and then apply the Gaussian Blur filter.

making it appear as though someone was shooting at a door, and the assailant behind it shot back.

Blood Splats

Blood splats are easy. For the most part, they're just alpha channel squirts using an airbrush. Although you might be able to get away with using a red-shaded blast pattern for blood, blood (or other liquids, for that matter) tends to splatter, drip, or bead. The splat patterns in *Wolfenstein* are simply a dark red, with the shape of the splat located in the TGA's alpha channel. (See Figure 2.23.)

This game utilizes a dozen or so decals, some of which are randomly sized, rotated, and scattered on floors and walls when you blow someone away. Here's a quick way to make one such decal:

Figure 2.23   ©2002 Id Software, Inc.
A typical blood splat in Wolfenstein. The splat shape is the white area in the TGA's alpha channel.

1. Start a new 512 × 512-pixel RGB image, with a transparent background. Fill it with a deep red, such as hex# 170000.

2. Start a new channel in the Channels palette. Select the Airbrush tool, and then select a Spatter 39 pixels brush or something similar. Set the Flow to 10 percent. Now randomly spray white around the image, trying not to streak too much. (See Figure 2.24.)

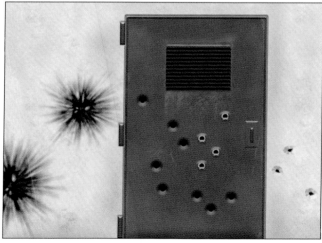

Figure 2.22
The blast mark and bullet hole decals being applied to a texture.

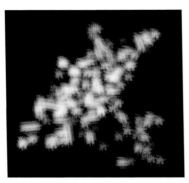

Figure 2.24
Create a new alpha channel and randomly spray a spatter brush in it.

3. To this channel, click Filter, Brush Strokes, Spatter. (See Figure 2.25.)

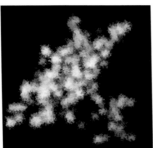

Filter: Brush Strokes, Spatter
Spray Radius: 10
Smoothness: 5

Figure 2.25
Apply the Spatter filter to the channel.

And that's it... Just resize your image (blood decals in *Wolfenstein* are either 128 × 128 or 64 × 64 pixels, depending on the application) and save it as a 32-bit TGA file. In Figure 2.26, the

Figure 2.26
The completed blood splatter decal in action.

blood splatter sprites are sprayed all over the scene. Check out the bones and guts of the guy I wasted.

Pipes

Pipes (as well as rivets and screws, and so on) can be considered decals because they're individual faux 3D elements on top of a texture, so I'll cover those here as well. These are the little details that can complete a texture; however, some of this stuff is good when done in 3D and then exported as a 2D image—especially things like elbow joints and couplings.

Basic Metal Pipes

Creating metal pipes is easy and effective. It's best to view your creations when the base layer is metal as well.

1. Start a new 512 × 512-pixel RGB image with a transparent background. Fill the background with black.

2. Create a new layer.

3. Using the Rectangular Marquee tool, create a selection that spans the width of the image. (See Figure 2.27.) This will be the pipe itself.

Figure 2.27
Create a rectangular selection in the shape of a pipe.

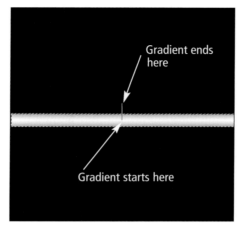

Figure 2.28
Add a reflected gradient to the selection.

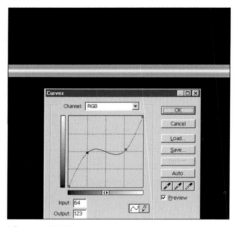

Figure 2.29
Adjust the levels or curves to enhance the pipe and make it shiny.

4. Press D to reset the swatches to black and white.

5. Click on the Gradient tool and, in the tool's options, select Reflected Gradient. (It's the button on top that looks like the top of a pipe.) Also enable the Reverse option.

6. Create a gradient, as shown in Figure 2.28. The gradient should start in the selection area's midpoint and extend upward beyond the selection; the total height of the gradient should be the same as the height of the selection. (It might help to press and hold down the Shift key when creating the gradient to keep the line snapped to 90 degrees.)

7. Press Ctrl+D to deselect the selected area.

8. Choose Image, Adjust, Levels, and slide the Shadows marker to the right a bit to darken the top and bottom edges of the pipe.

9. To enhance the pipe's shininess, adjust the curves as I have in Figure 2.29.

To quickly make a pipe fitting, do the following:

1. Create a small rectangular selection surrounding any portion of the pipe.

2. Right-click on the selection and choose Layer Via Copy.

3. Choose Edit, Transform, Scale, and scale the fitting so that it's slightly larger than the pipe.

4. Apply a slight drop shadow to the fitting's layer to complete the effect. (See Figure 2.30.)

Figure 2.30
Create a pipe fitting by copying and transforming a small portion of the base pipe.

Making pipes can get somewhat interesting. Try creating a pipe within a pipe, and then cut notches into the outer pipe to create a futuristic effect. On a layer below a pipe, put another pipe that is perpendicular to the first, and use the Elliptical Marquee tool to cut a semi-circle out of the base pipe (where the two pipes meet) to make them look joined. (See Figure 2.31.)

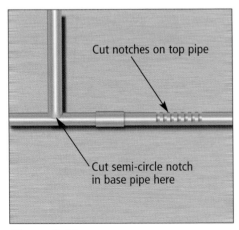

Figure 2.31
Adding joined pipes and other effects.

Bent Pipes

The Reflected Gradient tool is good only when you want to create a straight pipe; creating a similar effect on a curved pipe is somewhat more difficult. Here's how:

1. Start a new 512 × 512-pixel RGB image with a transparent background.

2. Fill the new image with any texture you like; here I'm using a simple metal texture, made by filling the background with the Noise filter and then applying the Motion Blur filter.

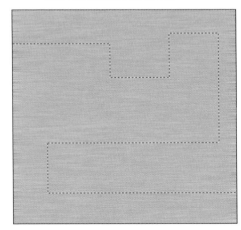

Figure 2.32
Use the Polygonal Lasso tool to make a selection that your pipe will follow.

3. Enable Photoshop's Snap and Grid features.

4. Use the Polygonal Lasso tool to create a selection for your pipe to follow. Figure 2.32 is mine.

5. Create a new channel in the Channels palette.

6. Choose Edit, Stroke, and stroke the center of the selection with white, about 25 pixels. The thicker your stroke, the thicker the pipe will be. (See Figure 2.33.)

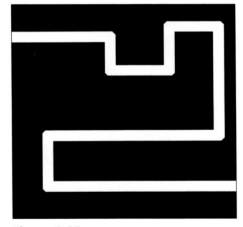

Figure 2.33
Stroke the selection with white in a new channel.

7. Press Ctrl+D to deselect the selection.

8. Still with the new channel open, choose Filter, Blur, Gaussian Blur (about 7.0 pixels).

9. Choose Image, Adjust, Levels, and pull the Shadows and Highlights markers together to make the image crisper. This creates rounded corners. (See Figure 2.34.) The pipe is starting to come into view.

Filter: Blur, **Gaussian Blur Radius:** 7.0 pixels

Figure 2.34
Apply a Gaussian Blur to the channel, and then adjust the levels to sharpen it.

10. Now that you have a rounded-edge selection, let's bring the pipe back. Ctrl+click the channel to load the selection, and apply the Gaussian Blur filter again. Having the selection

loaded constrains the blur to the selection boundary.

11. Press Ctrl+C to copy the pixels in the selection.

12. In the Layers palette, paste (Ctrl+V) the copied pixels. (See Figure 2.35.)

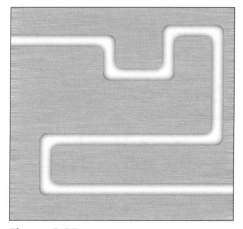

Figure 2.35
Load the channel's selection and apply the Gaussian Blur filter again. Copy and paste this selection into the Layers palette.

13. Desaturate the new bent pipe layer by choosing Image, Adjust, Desaturate. This causes the colors to revert to grayscale.

14. Adjust the levels and curves like you did in the earlier section "Basic Metal Pipes," and add a

drop shadow. In Figure 2.36, I crowned it off by enlarging the elbows and adding some end fittings to give the corners that "elbow pipe" look.

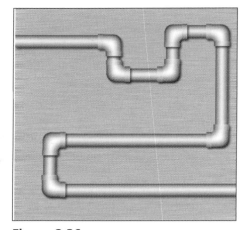

Figure 2.36
Desaturate the layer, and adjust the levels and curves. Add a drop shadow and fittings to complete the bent pipe.

Adding Some Realism to the Pipes

Maintaining a flow from the end of the previous exercise, you can quickly add to the pipes a mask of sorts that makes them appear a bit more real, as though they are tarnished and worn. This is typical of nearly every texture I make, and I use this procedure often.

Objects in video games rarely look "brand new"; they all have something of a tattered look to them.

1. Picking up from the previous step 14, with your pipe (and fittings and whatnot) on a separate layer from the background, Ctrl+click the pipe layer to select the entire pipe and fittings.

2. Start a new layer above the pipe layer.

3. Press D to reset the Color Control Panel. With the selection still active, choose Filter, Render, Clouds. Now choose Filter, Render, Difference Clouds a few times. Finally, choose Filter, Noise, Add Noise, about 10 percent. (See Figure 2.37.)

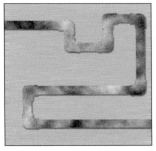

Filter: Noise, **Add Noise Amount:** 10% **Distribution:** Gaussian **Monochromatic:** (checked)

Figure 2.37
Select the entire pipe layer and apply Clouds, Difference Clouds, and Noise.

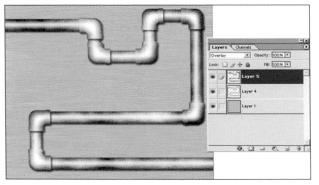

Figure 2.38
Change the cloud/noise layer's blending mode to Overlay to complete the effect.

4. In the Layers palette, change the blending mode of this cloud/noise layer to Overlay. Alternatively, try changing it to Darken with a 50-percent opacity. (See Figure 2.38.)

Rivets and Screws

Rivets and screws are just about the same thing, and they are fairly simple to create. If I were you, I'd set up a handful of actions to automatically generate different types of rivets and screws.

1. Start a new 512 × 512-pixel RGB image with a transparent background.

2. Fill the background with some type of metal texture.

3. Start a new layer.

4. Use the Elliptical Marquee tool to make a circular selection, about the size of a silver dollar, on your screen. (See Figure 2.39.) Holding down both Ctrl and Shift while creating the marquee makes the circle uniform.

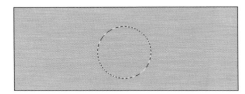

Figure 2.39
Create a circular selection on a new layer.

5. Set your foreground to medium-gray, such as hex# 808080, and set your background to pure white.

6. Select the Gradient tool. In the tool's options, choose Radial Gradient.

7. Create an angled gradient so that a white spot appears at the upper-left or upper-right portion of the circle. (See Figure 2.40.)

note

Bear in mind the overall direction of light being cast on your textures when you add these rivets and screws. Rotate the rivets to match that direction. It's good to make several versions of the same thing featuring light being received from different angles so that you have options of more suitable objects to place in your scene.

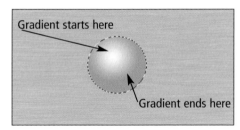

Figure 2.40
Add a radial gradient to the circle using medium-gray and white colors.

tip

If you want, you can adjust the levels or curves to enhance the rivet's shininess.

8. This could pass as a rivet head as it is, but I'd like to take it one step further. Apply an inner bevel with a cone contour to give it extra 3D curvature. (See Figure 2.41.)

note

Note the style parameters I've set in the Settings dialog box; if you play around with the function curve of the cone contour, you can achieve better results, but that's probably not necessary.

Style: Bevel and Emboss
Style: Inner Bevel
Technique: Smooth
Depth: 21%
Direction: Up
Size: 87 pixels
Soften: 0
Style: Contour
Figure 2.41 **Contour Shape:** Cone
Apply an inner **Range:** 50%
bevel with
contour to
polish it off.

9. You can finalize the effect in a couple of ways. One way is to add a simple drop shadow to make it look flush with the metal panel. Alternatively, you can add a blank layer between

the background and the rivet, link and merge the two to flatten the rivet's layer but retain the style, and then apply an outer bevel with a contour to make the rivet look like it's been tightened down firmly and is warping the metal. Figure 2.42 shows both types.

Style: Bevel and Emboss
Style: Outer Bevel
Technique: Smooth
Depth: 100%
Figure 2.42 **Direction:** Up
Add a drop shadow to **Size:** 16 pixels
complete the rivet, or **Soften:** 0
flatten out the rivet and **Style:** Contour
add an outer bevel with **Contour Shape:** Cone - Inverted
a contour for a realistic **Range:** 50%
effect.

10. Turning a rivet into a Phillips-head screw is just a matter of flattening the layer and then adding and beveling a dark cross. First insert a layer behind the rivet, link the two, and choose Layer, Merge Linked. This preserves the layer styles but keeps the rivet on its own layer.

11. Add a new layer on top of the rivet.

12. Use the Rectangular Marquee tool to select a vertical and a horizontal slot in the middle of the rivet.

13. Fill the selection with dark gray.

14. Apply an inner bevel to the cross to complete the effect. (See Figure 2.43.)

Style: Bevel and Emboss
Style: Inner Bevel
Technique: Smooth
Depth: 510%
Direction: Down
Size: 16 pixels
Soften: 0

Figure 2.43
Add a dark cross on a new layer, and apply an inner bevel to turn the rivet into a Phillips-head screw.

The rivets and screws will look much better after you've scaled them down to size. In the image shown in Figure 2.44, I added rivets to some of the elements of this texture, including the upper pipes, as well as adding some dripping rust from them. The pipes in this example were also made exactly like I did in the "Basic Metal Pipes" section from earlier. To add realism, I overlaid the pipes with a rusty texture set to Overlay. (I go more into rust effects in later chapters.)

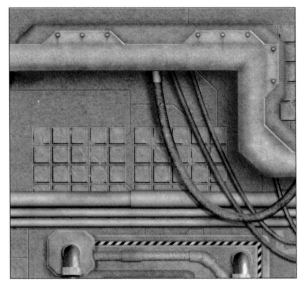

Figure 2.44
Scaling down the rivets and screws makes them look real. Add dripping-rust effects to crown it all off.

Peeling Paint on Metal

This one takes a little work, but I think you'll like it. In this tutorial, you'll add paint to a rusted-metal layer and then chip some of the paint away. You can then make this up as either a decal with an alpha channel to be placed on metal, or just an element within a texture.

1. Start a new 512 × 512-pixel RGB image with a transparent background.

2. Open the `basemetalrust.jpg` image located in the Chapter 2 folder on the CD-ROM. Once open, define a pattern with it by clicking Edit, Define Pattern. Then click Edit, Fill, and fill your image with this seamlessly tileable texture. (See Figure 2.45.)

Figure 2.45
Fill a new image with the `basemetalrust.jpg` texture.

3. Start a new layer.

4. Apply the Clouds filter with two dark yellow-green colors, such as hex# 5A4D2A and hex# 292718. (See Figure 2.46.) This represents paint.

Filter: Render, Clouds
Foreground:
hex#5A4D2A
Background:
hex#292718

Figure 2.46
Apply the Clouds filter on a new layer.

5. Make a copy of the paint layer.

6. With the copied layer selected, choose Filter, Noise, Add Noise (about 6 percent).

7. Set the Blending Mode of this layer to Color Dodge.

8. Merge the two paint layers. (See Figure 2.47.)

Filter: Noise, Add Noise
Amount: 6%
Distribution: Uniform
Monochromatic: (checked)
Blend Mode: Color Dodge

Figure 2.47
Copy the paint layer, add Noise, change the Blend mode to Color Dodge, and merge the layers.

9. Use the Lasso tool to create a curvy, closed selection that will represent where the paint has peeled away. (See Figure 2.48.)

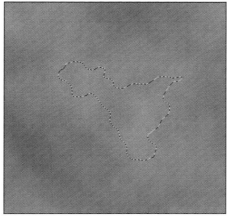

Figure 2.48
Use the Lasso tool to create a selection where the paint will be removed.

10. With the selection active, press Q to enter Quick Mask mode.

11. Choose Filter, Brush Strokes, Spatter to apply this filter to the mask.

Filter: Brush Strokes, Spatter
Spray Radius: 10
Smoothness: 5

Figure 2.49
Apply the Spatter filter to the selection in Quick Mask mode. Delete the selection from the paint layer.

12. Press Q again to exit the mask.

13. Press Delete to remove the paint. (See Figure 2.49.)

14. Using the Dodge tool at 25 percent exposure, dodge out highlights on all the areas where the paint curves in or creates tips. The highlights will eventually appear to make the paint peel upward.

15. Using the Burn tool at about 12 percent exposure, burn shadows a bit just behind the white portions you just dodged, as well as on the portions where the paint curves away from the inside. (See Figure 2.50.)

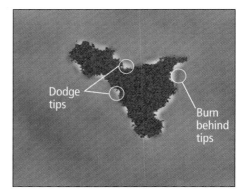

Dodge tips

Burn behind tips

Figure 2.50
Dodge and Burn highlights and shadows at key points around the paint's edges.

16. To the paint layer, apply an inner bevel and a drop shadow. (See Figure 2.51.)

Figure 2.51
Apply an inner bevel and a drop shadow to the paint layer.

Style: Bevel and Emboss
Style: Inner Bevel
Technique: Smooth
Depth: 81%
Direction: Down
Size: 8 pixels
Soften: 0
Highlight Mode: Screen, gray-green
Style: Drop Shadow
Distance: 7 pixels

Now you can flatten the image and isolate the peeling paint portion. Then you can either assign an alpha transparency to a new channel or just copy/paste it into a texture. In Figure 2.52, I put the peeling paint portion

Figure 2.52
Isolate the peeling paint area and use it on other textures, or make a decal out of it by assigning an alpha channel to the opaque areas.

on a sign and added bullet holes to it, making it appear that the sign started peeling and rusting because of the holes.

Signs

Signs are rectangular decals placed wherever the artist chooses. They can be with or without transparency depending on what the sign is—if it's a sprayed-on stencil or has rust that drips off of it and onto the wall behind it, then it has to have an alpha channel associated with it. If it's just an opaque sign, then it's a JPG file (unless, of course, the sign has rounded corners, in which case it, too, will need an alpha channel).

Dripping Decal

This quick one will be a typical spray-painted stencil decal seen in *Wolfenstein*. The sign is dripping from the rain over time. You can use the drip technique for rust as well, but sometimes just using the Smudge tool by hand works equally well.

1. Create a 512 × 512 RGB image with a transparent background. Fill the background with black.

2. Using the Type tool with something like an Arial Black font, create and scale some text as I have done in Figure 2.53. Center the text and move it up a bit to make room for the dripping effect below.

VERBOTEN

Figure 2.53
Make some text and leave room below it for the dripping effect.

3. Click Layer, Rasterize, Type. This converts the text from a vector-based image to ordinary pixels so that you can edit it directly.

4. Use the Line tool to create some vertical black lines of about 5 × 7 pixels wide through any letters with closed loops to simulate a stencil. (See Figure 2.54.) It helps to hold down the Shift key when drawing the lines to make it snap to 45-degree increments.

Figure 2.54
Use the Line tool to draw some vertical lines through the text to simulate a stencil pattern.

5. Ctrl+click the text layer to load its selection. Press Q to enter Quick Mask Mode. (See Figure 2.55.) This mode allows you to quickly edit an existing selection.

Figure 2.55
Load the text selection and enter Quick Mask Mode.

6. Press Ctrl+A to select the entire image. Click Edit, Transform, Rotate 90 Degrees Counter-Clockwise. (See Figure 2.56.) This moves the masked selection into position for the Wind filter.

Figure 2.56
Select the entire image and rotate it 90 degrees counterclockwise.

7. Choose Filter, Stylize, Wind. Make sure the wind direction comes from the left. Repeat this filter a few times to get the desired dripping length. (See Figure 2.57.)

8. Rotate the mask back by clicking Edit, Transform, Rotate 90 Degrees Clockwise. Press Q to exit Quick Mask Mode. You can now see the modified selection.

Filter: Stylize, Wind
Method: Wind
Direction: From the left

Figure 2.57
Apply the Wind filter, from the left, to create the dripping effect.

9. While keeping the dripping selection active, delete the top text layer. Create a new channel in the Channels palette, and fill this selection with white. (See Figure 2.58.) Kind of a creepy effect, yes?

Figure 2.58
Rotate the mask back to normal. Delete the text layer and fill the dripping selection with white in a new channel.

Now it's just a matter of cropping and resizing this sign; I cropped the text at 512 × 256 pixels, and then reduced it to 128 × 64 pixels, which is a proper size for the *Wolfenstein* game engine. I also dirtied up the text in the alpha channel so that the decal looked weathered. (See Figure 2.59.) Remember to save this as a 32-bit TGA file to retain the alpha channel.

Figure 2.59
Finish the decal by cropping and resizing it to fit into the game engine.

The dripping procedure is handy with odd-shaped items, especially when you need the effect to drip a long distance.

Stamped Metal Sign

This one makes clever use of an alpha channel along with the Lighting Effects filter to produce a metal sign with raised print, as if it were stamped by a license plate machine.

1. The base image here will be huge, allowing for better resolution and overall output. This is normally the type of size I like to work in; just keep the image at 33 percent while you work so that you can see everything. Create a new 1536 × 2048, 300 pixel-per-inch RGB image with a transparent background. Filters and other effects work well at this resolution.

2. Fill the image with a paint color blend. In Figure 2.60, I applied the Clouds and Difference Clouds filter several times, using deep red colors such as hex# 460000 and hex# 240000. Then apply the Noise filter at about 5 percent.

Figure 2.60
Fill the image with a deep red mix using the Clouds filters, and then add some noise.

3. Go to the Channels palette and create a new channel. You won't be using this channel as transparency information; rather, it will act as a displacement map for the Lighting Effects filter. Create and scale some text with the Type tool, and add anything else you want. In Figure 2.61, I added "not without authorization" in German, and some skull and crossbones, along with a thick border. The border gives a nice touch to the sign in the end.

Figure 2.61
Create a new channel and add some text, a border, and anything else you want. This channel will be a displacement map for the Lighting Effects filter.

4. Click Filter, Blur, Gaussian Blur, with a radius of about 3 pixels. Blurring this channel feathers the stamping effect. (That is, the roundness of the text is a direct function of how much blur is applied.) Don't blur too much; otherwise, the text and whatnot won't be discernable. (See Figure 2.62.)

Figure 2.62
Apply the Gaussian Blur filter with a radius of 3 pixels.

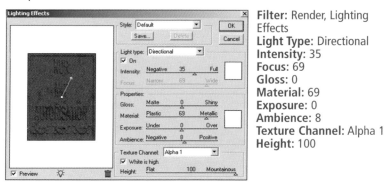

Figure 2.63
Select the base layer and apply the Lighting Effects filter using the Alpha 1 channel as a displacement map.

5. Go back to the Layers palette and click on the base layer. Click Filter, Render, Lighting Effects, using a Directional light source as I have done in Figure 2.63. In this filter, also choose Alpha 1 as the Texture Channel at the bottom, and slide the height to Mountainous.

tip

You can use the Lighting Effects filter to create many other textures by using an alpha channel as a displacement map. See Chapter 7, "Planetary Textures," where I use the Lighting Effects filter to create lava and rock textures.

6. After you've applied the filter, you should get a nice stamped metal texture like mine in Figure 2.64. You might have to undo the filter (Ctrl+Alt+Z) and readjust the alpha channel to get the proper results. When you're satisfied, adjust the levels of the image to your taste.

Filter: Render, Lighting Effects
Light Type: Directional
Intensity: 35
Focus: 69
Gloss: 0
Material: 69
Exposure: 0
Ambience: 8
Texture Channel: Alpha 1
Height: 100

Figure 2.64
The Lighting Effects filter applied to the base layer.

Figure 2.65
Create some additional effects by copying and pasting the peeling paint example from earlier. Set the blending mode of this new layer to Overlay.

Figure 2.66
The completed sign.

You could stop here, but I like to bang up the sign a bit. For instance, in Figure 2.65, I made a lasso selection around the "peeling paint on metal" example from before, and with the selection active, I chose Select, Feather, with a radius of 5 pixels. Then I pressed Ctrl+C to copy the selection, and I pasted it into the image. After scaling it to proper size, I set the blending mode of this new layer to Overlay, which blended it in nicely.

To complete the sign, I added some additional rust to it and marked it up here and there. Use the Spatter brushes in conjunction with the Burn tool for some of these effects. (See Figure 2.66.)

Wood Sign

In this example, I create a wooden sign in German and hang it on a castle wall. As with other textures, you can create wood in one of two ways: by taking a picture of the real thing, or by making it from scratch via filters. I've tried to re-create wood from scratch, but the best I've come up with is something that looks like those snap-together, faux-finish plastic pieces kids get for G.I. Joe karate boards.

If you did any of my Photoshop tutorials, the `sampler.psd` file had a piece of fake wood I made.

1. Start a new 512 × 512-pixel RGB image.

2. Fill the background layer with black.

3. Open the `woodpic.jpg` file in the Chapter 2 section on the CD-ROM. (See Figure 2.67.)

Figure 2.67
The `woodpic.jpg` image from which you'll extract some wood.

4. Using the Polygonal Lasso tool, select a board from the image, copy it, and paste it into a new layer. Repeat for a second board (pasting it into a new layer as well), as shown in Figure 2.68. Scale each board so that it fits in the image.

tip

You don't have to do a perfect job with the selection. In fact, it's better to keep your selection boundary within the border of the wood so that you don't have to clean up the edges.

Figure 2.68
Copy and paste two boards from the picture into your new image. (I'm using the two vertical boards on top.)

5. Rotate the two boards horizontally and align them so that they are parallel to each other with just a slight gap in between. (This is going to be a rustic old sign, so don't be too finicky.)

6. Merge the two board layers when finished. (See Figure 2.69.)

Figure 2.69
Rotate and align the boards with a slight gap.

7. Let's tear up and then apply a 3D effect to the left and right edges of the boards to give them some depth. Using the Lasso tool, make a jagged selection along the left edge and choose Layer Via Cut. As shown in Figure 2.70, my selection is only slightly inside the edge of the wood.

8. Move the new cut layer from the top of the layer stack to the middle.

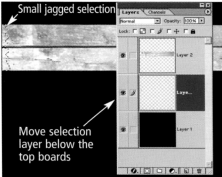

Figure 2.70
Make a jagged cut at the end of the boards onto a new layer. Position the layer between the other two.

9. Apply a drop shadow style to the top layer (the one with the boards).

10. In the jagged cut layer, use the Lasso tool to make *another* jagged cut to its outside border to match the inner jagged cut. Now the board's overall edge looks three dimensional and chopped up. (See Figure 2.71.)

Figure 2.71
Apply a drop shadow to the top boards, and cut up the edge to complete the 3D effect.

11. Repeat the jagged look for the right side of the board.

tip

Later on, you can use the Burn tool to further darken areas that stand out, particularly the sharp edges at the ends of the boards.

---

12. Link all layers except for the background layer, and choose Layer, Merge Linked.

13. Let's bind the two boards with a rusty iron binder. First, create a new layer.

14. On the new layer, use the Rectangular Marquee tool to create a selection near the left end that's slightly thicker than the two boards combined.

15. Fill the selection with the `basemetalrust.jpg` texture.

16. Apply a drop shadow to the binder with the same settings as before. (See Figure 2.72.)

Style: Drop Shadow
Blend Mode: Multiply
Opacity: 75%
Angle: 0 degrees
Distance: 0
Spread: 45
Size: 8

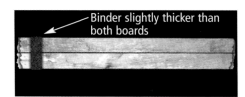

Figure 2.72
Make a rectangular selection on a new layer and fill it with the `basemetalrust.jpg` texture. This will be the metal that binds the two boards together.

17. On a new layer above the binder, add two rusty rivets using the Rivet procedure outlined earlier in this chapter.

18. Link and merge the rivet layer with the binder layer, and then copy it to the right side of the boards. (See Figure 2.73.)

19. Add and scale some dark text to the wood with a font of your choice. I masked and spattered my text selection using Filter, Brush Strokes, Spatter before filling it, to give it a weathered

Figure 2.73
Add rivets to the binder, and copy the binder to the right side.

> look. You'll have to be in Quick Mask Mode (press Q) to apply the filter to the selection, just like I showed you in the dripping decal earlier.

20. Apply a contoured outer bevel to recess the text into the wood.

21. Rasterize the type and cut out a selection where the gap between the boards exist. (See Figure 2.74.)

Figure 2.74
Add text to the wood and apply a contoured outer bevel. Split the text where the gap exists between the boards.

Because I'm going to put this sign on a castle wall, I added some dripping-rust effects from the iron binders and created an alpha channel for the transparency. (See Figure 2.75.) Also, add a drop shadow for the entire sign

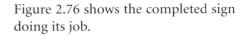

Figure 2.75
To prepare it for a game like *Wolfenstein*, I created an alpha channel (below) for the sign, so the dripping rust coming off of the binders will lay over a castle wall.

on a wall to give it depth, and use the Burn tool to burn out those annoying highlights everywhere.

Figure 2.76 shows the completed sign doing its job.

Summary

As you have seen, decals are simply miniature textures that are either statically or dynamically laid over existing textures in a game. These images are typically coupled with an alpha channel to relay to the game engine which areas of the image are transparent, semi-transparent, or opaque. In this chapter, I covered a variety of decals from static signs and texture elements like pipes, rivets, and screws,

Figure 2.76
The completed sign hanging on a castle wal.

to dynamic decals like blast marks and bullet holes that are applied actively during the game's pursuit. Not all game engines dictate the setup of decals in the same manner, so it is necessary to research the engine's documentation to determine the file setup of your decal so that it can display it properly. In this chapter, I provided specific examples of creating many of the decals for use in *Return to Castle Wolfenstein,* which utilizes the *Quake III* engine. There are other games that use this engine as well, such as *Soldier of Fortune II, Star Wars - Jedi Knight II: Jedi Outcast,* and *Star Trek: Elite Force.* Altering these decal examples for other game engines is usually just a matter of changing the transparency color, creating an alpha channel, or saving the file in a different format.

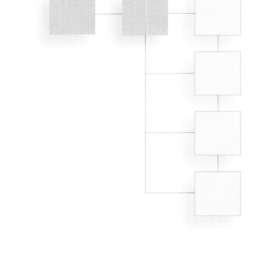

CHAPTER 3

SPRITES

Perpetuum mobile...

Something in perpetual motion...

Sprites, or animated textures, are 2D images that are either a sequence of files that make up an animation or a single texture that's animated by the game engine. These images usually have an alpha channel associated with them for transparency. Unless the game engine uses some type of particle system, sprites are an efficient and effective way to produce volumetric entities such as smoke, fire, lightning/electricity, and weapon discharges. Creating these animations requires certain software tools and is subject for another book; however, in this chapter, I will teach you the following:

- What the different types of sprites are and how they are used
- How to make sprite decals and animations
- How to view sprite animations in Adobe ImageReady
- How to create and apply a fire sprite animation in Photoshop and ImageReady, for use in *Return to Castle Wolfenstein*

Sprite Basics

Again, I'll be using *Return to Castle Wolfenstein* (*Wolfenstein*) to direct my examples in this chapter, but these can apply to any other game engine merely by changing the sprite parameters required by the engine in question. There are two basic types of sprites: sprite decals, which are single images that the game engine can animate via the use of scripts or shaders (a *shader* is a file that contains code to drive the vertices of a mesh object, such as making a water surface wavy); and sprite animations, which are a series of animation frames saved in separate images.

Sprite Decals

These are single images that usually find themselves in applications like lightning bolts and rocket flares. For instance, in *Wolfenstein*, the tesla gun would shoot several lightning bolts at once, arcing all over the place. The sprite, and the sprite in action, are shown in Figure 3.1. The game engine handles stretching and bending this image, and it uses the JPG's black areas to determine which areas are transparent.

tip

Using an alpha channel in a TGA file to tell the game engine what areas in the image are transparent gives you more direct control of the image's transparency. If the sprite doesn't look quite right in the game, alter the channel slightly to expose or hide pixels. JPG images force you to alter the image directly.

Figure 3.1   ©2002 Id Software, Inc.
A lightning bolt sprite decal shooting off the tesla gun in *Wolfenstein*.

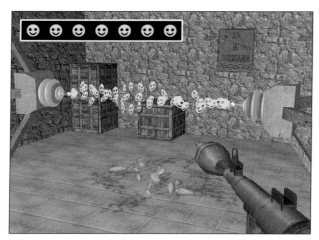

Figure 3.2
Here I've replaced a lightning bolt sprite with happy faces so that you can see what a typical game engine does to it.

In a moment, I'll show you how to make a lightning bolt sprite. Meanwhile, to show you what a typical game engine does with this type of sprite, I've replaced it with a happy-face pattern, seen in Figure 3.2.

Making a Lightning Bolt Sprite

Making the sprite by hand in Figure 3.1 isn't difficult; it's mostly a bluish-white scraggly line with an outer glow style applied to it. However, Photoshop offers a cool way to generate lightning using the Clouds filter.

tip

Record this procedure in the Actions palette. That way, you can quickly redo the image over and over until you get a lightning bolt pattern you like.

1. Start a new 1024 × 1024-pixel RGB image with a transparent background.

2. Press D to reset the Color Control Panel. Click Filter, Render, Clouds. Then click Filter, Render, Difference Clouds. (See Figure 3.3.)

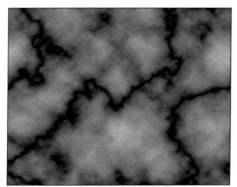

Figure 3.3
Fill a new image with the Clouds and Difference Clouds filters.

3. Click Image, Adjust, Invert. Your image will turn mostly white.

4. Click Image, Adjust, Levels, and slide the left Shadows marker most of the way to the right, until your lightning bolts come into focus. Leave them a bit fuzzy, as I have in Figure 3.4.

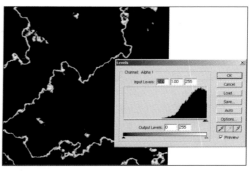

Figure 3.4
Invert the image and adjust the levels in the image until the lightning bolts come into focus.

5. Use the Lasso tool to select a fairly straight portion of one of the bolts. Copy this selection (Ctrl+C).

6. Start a new 512 × 64-pixel image, and fill the background with black.

7. Go to the Channels palette, create a new channel, and paste (Ctrl+V) the lightning bolt there. You might have to click Edit, Free Transform and scale and rotate the bolt so that it stretches from edge to edge like mine in Figure 3.5. You need to paste this into a new channel because we're interested in the white areas of the bolt.

Figure 3.5
Copy a long bolt using the Lasso tool and paste it into a channel in a new 512 × 64-pixel image.

8. Ctrl+click the channel to load the lightning bolt selection.

9. Go back to the Layers palette and start a new layer. With the selection still active, press D and then X to set the foreground color to white, and then press Alt+Backspace to fill the selection with white. The bolt is now isolated on its own layer.

10. Double-click the bolt layer to open the Styles panel, and apply light blue Outer Glow. (See Figure 3.6.)

Figure 3.6
Load the bolt selection and fill it with white on a new layer. Apply a light blue Outer Glow style to it.

There you have it! In Figure 3.7, I saved this image as `lightning.jpg` and placed it in a game. If you want to replace the tesla gun's sprite in *Wolfenstein*, open the `pak0.pk3` file and place this file in the \SPRITES directory. The bolts will look just fine coming out of the tesla gun.

caution

Remember to make a backup of the `pak0.pk3` file before modifying it. That way, you can always revert to the backup copy if the file becomes corrupted.

There are dozens of such sprites in this game. If you shoot a machine gun, the smoke puffs that float away from the bullet holes are a single sprite image; the stream of fire coming out of the

Style: Outer Glow
Blend Mode: Screen
Opacity: 75%
Noise: 0
Color: hex# 0095FD
Technique: Softer
Spread: 5%
Size: 16 pixels
Range: 50%
Jitter: 0%

flamethrower is a single sprite, and so on.

Sprite Animations

In *Return to Castle Wolfenstein* or most other 3D games, when you use

Figure 3.7
The new lightning bolt sprite in action in the same game from Figure 3.2.

Figure 3.8   ©2002 Id Software, Inc.
An explosion sprite animation in *Wolfenstein*, emanating from a grenade I threw.

Figure 3.9   ©2002 Id Software, Inc.
You can view the entire explosion animation sequence in Photoshop ImageReady.

why the explosion looks the same each time. Note that I'm displaying only 12 of the actual 24 frames that comprise the entire animation.

something like a grenade or rocket-propelled grenade (Panzerfaust), the resulting explosion is a sprite animation. (See Figure 3.8.) The animation consists of a dozen or so TGA files, which are a frame-by-frame extrapolation from an explosion video clip. Each of the files carries with it an alpha channel to represent the transparent areas that surround the fireball.

The animation here is placed on a 2D plane, which increases proportionally in size with each frame to make the fireball grow. This plane always faces perpendicular to the player, which is

Using ImageReady to View Animations

ImageReady is a sister program that's packaged along with Photoshop. It is used primarily to prepare content for the Internet, including GIF animations. To view the full animation from Figure 3.8, go to ImageReady by clicking on the bottom button of the toolbar in Photoshop or by pressing Ctrl+Shift+M. Then click File, Import, Folder as Frames, and browse to a folder containing an animation sequence. The animation displayed in Figure 3.8 is located in the pak0.pk3 file, in the \SPRITES\EXP-BLUE directory. ImageReady displays the entire sequence frame by frame, allowing you to play it or preview it in Internet Explorer. (See Figure 3.9.)

You can also save it as a GIF file by clicking File, Save Optimize As.

Obviously, you can view other games' sprite animations; it's a matter of extracting the sprite textures from their texture package files.

Creating an Explosion

The best explosions are real ones, videotaped at night or against a black background. You can search the Web and find lots of downloadable AVI files of explosions and other effects. Nowadays, however, 3D modeling and animation software like 3D Studio Max have become so powerful that you can quickly create realistic explosions, flames, and fireballs in just minutes. Max carries an expensive price tag ($2,500), but it's well worth it. Because this is a Photoshop book, I'm not going to present a tutorial on explosions with a 3D modeling program. Again, just search the Web, and you'll find lots of such tutorials.

Creating a Fire Sprite in Photoshop

Creating animations in Photoshop is easy but takes a bit of effort. You can create an explosion as well, but that would warrant a good deal of planning. In *Wolfenstein*, you'll often see fire sprites in action. Bonfires, window fires, and so on are everywhere, and they're usually the same sprite animation. (See Figure 3.10.) These sprites are placed on a 2D plane as

Figure 3.10   ©2002 Id Software, Inc.
Fire sprites in *Wolfenstein*. Note that they are placed on a couple of 2D planes to give the fire a volumetric look.

well and, in many cases, there are multiple, crossed planes to give the fire volume. These planes don't usually face the player, so you can view them from all sides.

Follow these steps to create your own fire animation:

1. The fire sprite used in *Wolfenstein* consists of eight 64 × 128-pixel TGA files, each with an alpha channel to represent the transparency information. Let's work large and reduce; therefore, create a 512 × 1024-pixel RGB color image with a transparent background. Fill it with pure black.

2. Create a new layer. Using the Brush tool with a 100-pixel soft round brush, set the brush flow to 20 percent and gently spray a small white cloud near the bottom. This represents the base of the fire.

3. Select the Smudge tool, with a strength of about 80 percent, and create spires out of the cloud, as I have done in Figure 3.11.

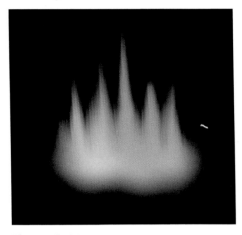

Figure 3.11
In a new image, spray a small, white cloud near the bottom with the Brush tool. Then create spires using the Smudge tool.

4. Click Edit, Transform, Scale, and scale up the fire so that it fills a good 75 percent of the image. (See Figure 3.12.)

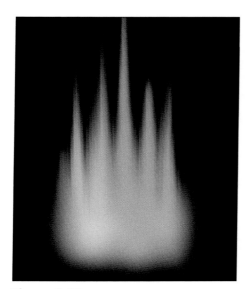

Figure 3.12
Scale up the fire so that it fills 75 percent of the image.

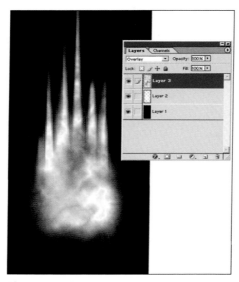

Figure 3.13
Break up the fire with a Clouds/Difference Clouds layer, set to Overlay.

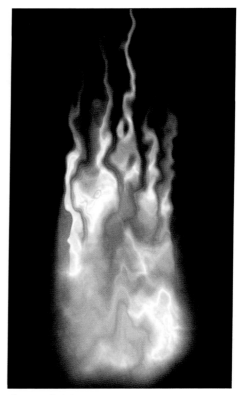

Figure 3.14
Make the fire pattern look more real by using the Turbulence tool in the Liquify filter.

5. Create a new layer. Set this layer's blending mode to Overlay. Press D to reset the Color Control Panel, and then click Filter, Render, Clouds. Click Filter, Render, Difference Clouds a few times, and then click Image, Adjust, Invert. (See Figure 3.13.) This effectively breaks up the image.

6. Click Layer, Flatten Image to merge the layers down.

7. Click Filter, Liquify (Ctrl+Shift+X). A new feature in Photoshop 7's Liquify filter is the Turbulence tool, which is second from the top on the left (three wavy lines on a button). Enable that tool and use it to add turbulence to the spires. (See Figure 3.14.) When you're satisfied, click OK.

8. Click Image, Adjust, Variations. This is a great tool to quickly change the colors in your image. In Figure 3.15, I clicked on More Yellow and More Red a few times each to get some nice fire colors.

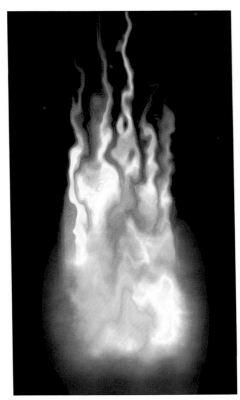

Figure 3.15
Use the Variations adjustment to change
the fire colors to yellow-red.

9. Create a new layer and set its
blending mode to Color Burn.

10. Press D to make sure your colors are black and white. Fill the
new layer with the Clouds filter,
and then apply the Difference

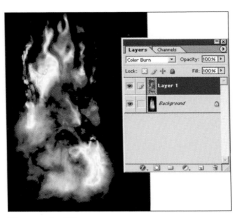

Figure 3.16
Apply the Clouds/Difference Clouds filters
on a new layer. Set this layer's blending
mode to Color Burn.

Clouds filter several times or
until you get a nice fiery look
like mine in Figure 3.16.

11. This top layer is the animation
mask we'll use to create the animation. Try moving the top
layer up and down, and you'll
see how it makes the fire come
alive. (Totally cool, huh?)

12. Adjust the levels of this layer
a bit to darken it. This hides
the fire some more so that it
doesn't stand out all over the
place. (See Figure 3.17.)

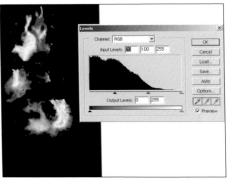

Figure 3.17
Adjust the levels of the top layer to darken
the fire.

13. We need to have this top layer
doubled in height so that it can
travel a bit during the animation without moving offscreen.
Temporarily hide the bottom
layer by clicking its "eye" icon in
the Layers palette. Then move
the top layer down so that the
top edge of the image is in the
middle of the screen. Make a
copy of this layer and move it
until the two layers meet and
blend perfectly together. Notice
that this is possible because the
Clouds filters automatically create seamless images.

14. Merge these top two cloud layers. You should now have one

layer on top of the bottom fire layer. The top layer should be twice as long as the bottom. Move down this entire strip until the top edge is aligned with the top of the image. (This will be the starting point of the animation.) You can now unhide the bottom layer.

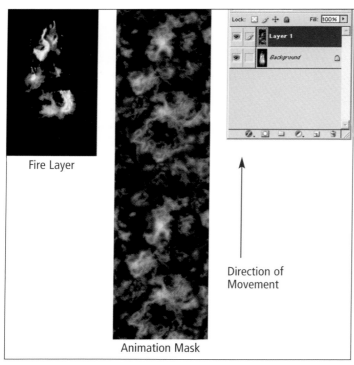

Fire Layer

Direction of Movement

Animation Mask

Figure 3.18
The completed fire sprite ready for animation.

15. Figure 3.18 demonstrates what you should have now. It represents the completed fire sprite that is ready for animation in ImageReady.

Animating the Fire Sprite in ImageReady

Now we're ready to create the actual animation. As you can see, we'll make the animation by moving the top layer slowly upward. The blending mode, in combination with the cloudy layer, dictates which portions of the fire are masked and which are revealed. Image-Ready handles the actual animation by *tweening*, or filling in the frames between the endpoints of the animation. All we have to do is create a start and an end.

1. You can leave the image size the way it is if you want, but to prepare it for *Return to Castle Wolfenstein*, click Image, Image Size, and resize it to 128 × 256 pixels. This is the same size of the existing animation in the game.

2. Enter ImageReady by clicking on the bottom button on the toolbar or by pressing Ctrl+Shift+M.

3. If the Animation palette is not visible, click Window, Animation. This palette shows a frame-by-frame display of the current animation. There will only be a single frame here now, which is frame 1, or the beginning of the entire sequence. (See Figure 3.19.)

Figure 3.19
Switch to ImageReady and view the first frame of the animation in the Animation palette.

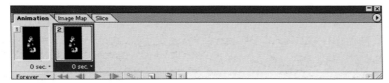

Figure 3.20
Copy the first frame by clicking the Duplicates Current Frame button. This represents the end frame of the animation sequence.

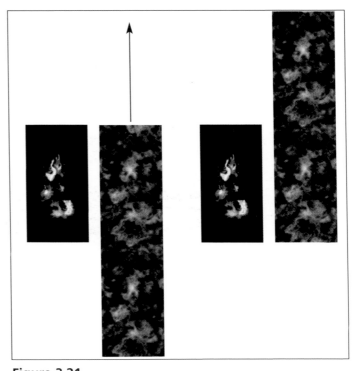

Figure 3.21
Create the end key frame by moving the top layer up about one full height of the image.

4. Click on the first frame of the animation, and then click the Duplicates Current Frame button located at the bottom of the Animation palette. This is the end of the animation sequence. (See Figure 3.20.)

5. Create the end key frame of the animation by selecting the top layer in the Layers palette and moving it up about one full height of the image. Figure 3.21 illustrates this concept. ImageReady can then tween the frames between the first and second frames by analyzing what has changed between the two frames.

6. Click on the original, first frame of the animation to make it active.

7. We'll need to create six more frames to complete the animation because the fire animation in *Wolfenstein* is eight frames. To create the tweens between the first and second frames, click on the Tweens Animation Frames button at the bottom of the Animation palette. This brings up the Tween screen.

8. In the Frames to Add area, enter a value of 6 and press OK. ImageReady generates all the animation frames between the

Figure 3.22
Create six tweened images by clicking the Tweens Animation Frames button to complete the animation.

first and last ones. (See Figure 3.22.) You can play the animation in the Animation palette by pressing the Play/Stop Animation button. It will be fast, though; *Wolfenstein* plays the animation much slower. You can create a much slower, smoother burning fire animation by entering a value of 30 or 60 in the Tween screen.

tip

Remember that I'm demonstrating this animation to replace a sprite in *Return to Castle Wolfenstein*. This animation can be made for any other game, with more frames for a smoother play. Consult the game engine's documentation to determine the proper sprite parameters.

9. Now the animation is complete. To get this to work in *Wolfenstein*, you need to manually save each frame as a TGA file. Click on the first frame of the animation, and then click File, Export Original. Save each frame as `flame1.tga`, `flame2.tga`, `flame3.tga`, and so on.

10. Finally, switch back over to Photoshop. You need to add transparency information to *each* of the TGA files you just saved. Do this by opening each file and, in the Channels palette, Ctrl+click the RGB channel to load the flame's selection. ImageReady probably created a blank alpha channel; just delete it. Create a new channel, and with the selection

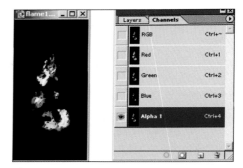

Figure 3.23
Create an alpha channel for each of the TGA files to indicate the transparency information of the animation.

still active, Alt+Backspace about seven times to fill it in with white. Doing it this many times ensures a proper transparency channel. (See Figure 3.23.) When you're finished, save the file and repeat for the other seven files.

You're done! Just replace the eight TGA files within the `pak0.pk3` file in the \TEXTURES\SFX directory. It helps to use a program like PakScape to do this. You can see this fire sprite in action in Figure 3.24.

Figure 3.24
The fire sprite blazing away in a game.

Summary

Sprites are 2D images that are either put into motion in a game, such as sprite decals, or they're a string of images that comprise a full animation. From smoke to fire, explosions, lightning, and weapon discharges, sprites simulate particle systems to save on the processing performance of computers.

In this chapter, I reviewed the different kinds of sprites and how they are used, particularly for *Return to Castle Wolfenstein*. Sprites can be as easy to make as a single image of a lightning bolt, or they can be complex, such as an explosion, which typically requires video footage or artificial creation in special 3D rendering software such as 3D Studio Max. In this chapter, I demonstrated how to make a realistic fire animation using Photoshop and its sister program, ImageReady, in a couple dozen steps. You can easily place an animation such as this in most game engines. It worked nicely in *Wolfenstein*.

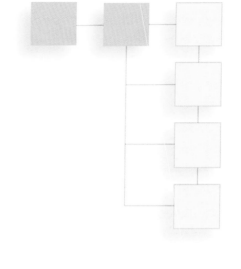

CHAPTER 4

MILITARY TEXTURES

Caveat emptor…

An event that causes or justifies war…

Semper fidelis…

Always faithful…(motto of the United States Marine Corps)

This is one of a few major topics in game texturing in which so many textures can be created based on only a handful of photographs of metal, wood, or cement surfaces. Here, I'll show you how to create some military-style textures, both from scratch using Photoshop's default filters as well as using photographs to create base textures. I'll also introduce you to creating textures based on a 3D model's U-V map (texture coordinate map), which represents the "skin" of the model.

You'll find that many times throughout this book, I'll first demonstrate how to create a texture completely from scratch, using nothing but a bunch of filters and some painting techniques. I do this not only because it's fun, but also so that you can see how far you can get using only Photoshop. It's actually surprising how realistic images can be, having been made solely with Photoshop; however, I'll always follow up with the latter, more proficient way of creating texture images via photograph.

In this chapter, I'll show you how to create the following:

- Base metal textures using Photoshop's filters
- Metal panels derived from base metal, as well as from photos
- Munitions crates made from scratch using Photoshop's filters
- Munitions crates made from photos
- A camouflage canvas texture made from scratch that you can use to cover your crates
- A complete texture skin for an RPG7-B grenade launcher 3D model, based on its U-V texture map

Metal Panels

In this section, I'll cover some basic techniques to create two metal panel textures. The first will be a metal panel made from scratch in only a few steps, and from that, I'll demonstrate a basic panel with multiple beveled panel insets. The next will be from scratch—a more realistic image that you can apply to something like a munitions box. Keep in mind that these examples only need slight altering to be appropriately applied to thousands of other models.

Base Metal Texture from Scratch

This is a simple filter-based brushed metal procedure that you can apply to any object requiring a finished metal look, such as a control panel or elevator doors.

1. Start a new 600 × 600-pixel RGB image. (You'll reduce it to 512 × 512 pixels on the last step to get rid of the smearing effect.)

2. Set your foreground color to a medium gray, such as hex# A7A6A6. Press Alt+Backspace to fill the canvas with it.

3. Choose Filter, Noise, Add Noise (about 25 percent), as shown in Figure 4.1.

Filter: Noise, Add Noise
Amount: 25%
Distribution: Uniform
Monochromatic: (checked)

Figure 4.1
Fill the image with gray and apply the Add Noise filter.

Filter: Blur, Motion Blur
Angle: 0 degrees
Distance: 50 pixels

Figure 4.2
Apply the Motion Blur filter.

4. Choose Filter, Blur, Motion Blur (about 50 pixels), as shown in Figure 4.2.

See the smearing/streaking that's going on at the left and right edges? Crop it by clicking Image, Canvas Size, and entering 512 for both the width and height. Now you have basic metal.

Military Panel #1

You can use the base metal texture in the previous section to create fairly realistic metal panels. This example could end up on the side of some military equipment, generator, or even a spaceship hull.

1. Start a new 512 × 512-pixel RGB image.

Filter: Render, Clouds
Foreground: hex# 141A00
Background: hex# 292602

Figure 4.3
Apply the Clouds filter using two dark green colors.

2. Apply the Clouds filter with two dark military-green colors such as hex# 141A00 and hex# 292602. (See Figure 4.3.)

3. Start a new layer.

4. Apply the entire Base Metal procedure you learned earlier to the new layer.

5. Set the layer's Blend mode to Soft Light. (See Figure 4.4.) This gives the overall texture a painted-steel look.

6. Merge the two layers.

7. Enable Photoshop's Snap and Grid features.

8. Using the Polygonal Lasso tool, create a shape that will become a panel. (See Figure 4.5.)

Figure 4.4
Add a new layer and apply the Base Metal procedure. Set its Blend mode to Soft Light.

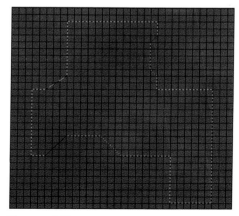

Figure 4.5
Use the Polygonal Lasso tool to create a shape that will become a panel.

9. Panels like this generally have curved edges. With the selection still active, go to the Channels palette and create a new channel.

10. Fill the selection with white.

11. Press Ctrl+D to deselect the selection.

12. Choose Filter, Blur, Gaussian Blur, with a radius of about 3.0 pixels.

13. Use the Levels dialog box to sharpen the white area, and then Ctrl+click the channel to select the panel's opacity. (See Figure 4.6.)

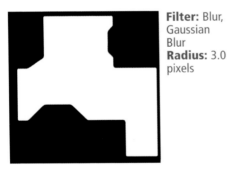

Filter: Blur, Gaussian Blur
Radius: 3.0 pixels

Figure 4.6
Fill the selection in a new channel, apply the Gaussian Blur filter, and adjust the levels to sharpen it.

14. With the revised selection loaded, go back to the Layers palette and select the painted-metal layer.

15. Press Ctrl+J (Layer Via Copy) to copy the metal within the selection boundary.

16. To this new layer, apply an inner bevel with an inverted-cone contour. (See Figure 4.7.) Adding the contour gives the panel a recessed look.

Style: Bevel and Emboss
Style: Inner Bevel
Technique: Smooth
Depth: 100%
Direction: Up
Size: 5 pixels
Soften: 0
Style: Contour
Contour Shape: Cone - Inverted
Range: 50%

Figure 4.7
Apply an inner bevel with contour to the metal panel.

17. Repeat steps 8 through 16 to add more panels. Then drag and drop the bevel effect from the first panel's layer onto the new ones. (See Figure 4.8.)

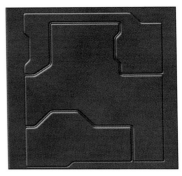

Figure 4.8
Add more panels to the scene using the same beveling effects as before.

18. If you want, you can link all the panel layers and merge them. This declutters your Layers palette.

19. To add a cool paint effect, begin by selecting a light yellow-green foreground color, such as hex# C3C44E, to be the paint color.

20. Using the Text tool, type some text, preferably in a large font.

21. When you're finished, scale the type appropriately, and choose Layer, Rasterize, Type to make it editable. (See Figure 4.9.)

Figure 4.9
Add text to the panels and then rasterize the type to make it editable.

22. Ctrl+click the text layer to load the text's opacity as a selection.

23. Choose Select, Inverse.

24. Press Q to enter Quick Mask mode.

25. Choose Filter, Brush Strokes, Spatter to apply the Spatter filter to the mask. This chops it up.

26. Press Q again to exit Quick Mask mode.

27. Press Delete. Now the text has a bit of a worn look. (See Figure 4.10.)

Figure 4.10
Select the text and use the Spatter filter in Quick Mask mode to chop it up.

Try using the Dodge and Burn tools to add more realism to the edges and whatnot. In Figure 4.11, I also added some inset hex screws to the corners, as well as some sustained shell damage. The techniques you use to create the holes are similar to creating the bullet holes in Chapter 2, "Nasty Decals." I dodged/burned the edges of

the holes to make the metal look fatigued. Remember to use a low exposure setting on these tools and to take your time.

Filter: Brush Strokes, Spatter
Spray Radius: 10
Smoothness: 10

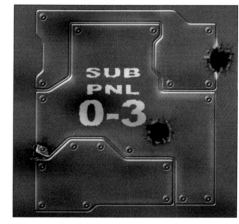

Figure 4.11
Add details to the texture to enhance realism.

Base Metal Texture from Photo

As I mentioned at the beginning of this chapter, using a photograph to create a base texture is the preferred

Figure 4.12
The `metalpanel.jpg` image located on the CD-ROM. This image will be used as the basis for creating a munitions crate panel.

Figure 4.13
Copy a 512 × 256-pixel selection from the image and paste it into a new canvas. Adjust the levels to darken.

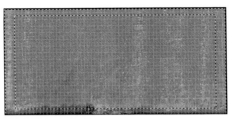

Figure 4.14
Start creating reinforcement ribs around the edge of the image by creating two rectangular selections. Use the Grid and Snap features to aid in the selection.

method of texturing in the digital art industry. Here I'll show you how I took a picture of the side of an electrical junction box to create a munitions crate panel.

Military Panel #2

To follow along with this exercise, open the `metalpanel.jpg` file located on the CD-ROM. (See Figure 4.12.) As you can see, the side of this junction box has lots of intricate detail—including faded paint and rust—that's generally difficult to reproduce from scratch. Obtaining the completed panel is a matter of making a small selection from the image and getting Photoshop to do the rest.

1. With the `metalpanel.jpg` image opened, create a 512 × 256-pixel selection somewhere in the image. I chose the bottom center, right where the rust begins. I figured that the rust would look good at the base of the munitions box, as if the thing had been sitting around for some time. (See Figure 4.13.) Ironically, there's nothing uglier than pretty, clean textures, so grabbing some filth from images is key.

When you've made your selection, copy it and paste it into a new canvas. In Figure 4.13, I've adjusted the levels a bit to darken the image. Most textures usually end up pretty

dark; unfortunately, I can only darken images a certain amount or they'll look near-black on print.

2. Metal munitions panels (such as ammo and weapons boxes) have punched reinforcement ribs that typically circumvent the edges of the panels as well as span across their centers once or several times. In Figure 4.14, I began this process by turning on the Grid and Snap features in Photoshop and making two rectangular selections on the border of the image.

Figure 4.15
Copy the selection to a new layer and apply a Drop Shadow style to give it depth.

Figure 4.16
Add another center rib and rivets around the reinforcement.

Figure 4.17
Finish the texture by adding some text, and create handles using the same technique that you used to create the reinforcement ribs.

3. With the selection active, right-click on it and choose Layer via Copy. To this new layer, apply a Drop Shadow style. In Figure 4.15, I made the shadow spread outward from all edges, giving the border some depth.

4. In Figure 4.16, I added another reinforcement rib up the center, as well as another drop shadow style. Also, I used the background layer to create rivets around the ribs. (See Chapter 2 for information on creating rivets and screws.)

5. To complete the image, try adding some text and handles. In Figure 4.17, I found a stencil font on the Web and typed in some black text, rasterized it, and faded it using the Eraser tool with a low pressure setting. The handles were created in almost the same way as the reinforcement ribs—just make handle-shaped selections using the Lasso tools, based on the background layer, and apply Inner Bevel styles to them. Make the handles float above the metal by applying a Drop Shadow style. Complete the entire texture by flattening it and adjusting the levels, curves, or Hue/Saturation to suit.

tip

Finishing textures to get the color, brightness, and whatnot correct always takes some trial and error. Sometimes you might have to force a texture using the Channel Mixer; for instance, in this texturing example, try setting the mixer's Output Channel to green, and play around with the sliders. This effectively adjusts the green portion of the image to your liking.

I continued using the same base photograph to create side and top panels to complete a munitions crate. Figure 4.18 shows the completed crate rendered in *trueSpace 6*.

Figure 4.18
The munitions crate texture rendered in *trueSpace 6*.

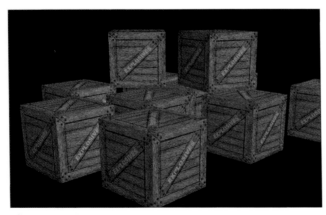

Figure 4.19
The texture we'll create in this section. Not a safe room to be in, eh?

Explosives Crate

This is a standard but useful prop that typically adorns those big empty rooms found on loads of game levels out there. To make a crate, I would typically just grab wood samples from images, but I'll show you how to do this one entirely from scratch. Figure 4.19 shows the completed crate texture, applied to 3D crate objects.

1. Start a new 512 × 512-pixel RGB color image.

2. Set Resolution to 512.

3. Activate Photoshop's Grid and Snap features by choosing View, Show, Grid (Ctrl+Alt+') and choosing View, Snap (Ctrl+;).

4. Choose Edit, Preferences, Guides and Grid and configure the grid in increments of 64 pixels. This represents the width of the boards on the crate texture.

5. Set your foreground and background to medium and dark browns, such as hex# 7C5004 and hex# 492A03, respectively.

6. With the background layer active, choose Filter, Render, Clouds.

7. Choose Filter, Noise, Add Noise, about 5 percent.

8. Choose Filter, Noise, Median, 1 pixel. (See Figure 4.20.) This represents the base of the wood texture.

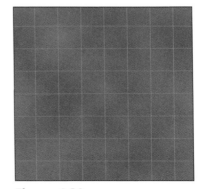

Figure 4.20
Fill the background with the Clouds filter, using medium and dark brown colors. Add some noise to break it up.

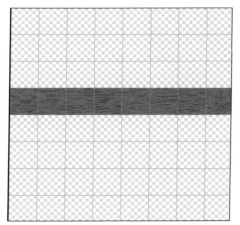

Filter: Sketch, Graphic Pen
Stroke Length: 15
Light/Dark Balance: 80
Stroke Direction: Horizontal

Figure 4.21
Copy the selection to a new layer and
apply the Graphic Pen filter.

9. Using the Rectangular Marquee
    tool, create a selection across
    the image that's only one 64-
    pixel cell wide. This will be our
    board shape.

10. Right-click on this selection
    and choose Layer Via Copy. The
    board is now on a separate
    layer.

11. With the new layer active,
    choose Filter, Sketch, Graphic
    Pen. In Figure 4.21, I've hidden
    the background layer to show
    you the results.

12. The image already looks like
    wood, but let's make the surface
    look a bit more three dimen-
    sional, using the wood as a dis-
    placement map. Ctrl+click the
    board's layer to load its selec-
    tion, and press Ctrl+C to make
    a copy of it.

13. In the Channels palette, start a
    new channel.

14. Press Ctrl+V to paste the
    copied selection. This will be
    the texture channel you'll use
    for the Lighting Effects filter in
    a moment. (See Figure 4.22.)
    (Note that the channel is black
    and white; the lighter areas rep-
    resent the higher portions,
    whereas the darker areas are
    recessed.)

15. Select the Layer 1 channel in
    the Layers palette. This should
    be the isolated board's layer.

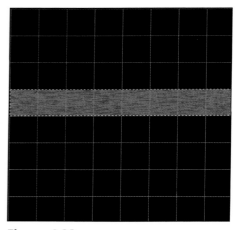

Figure 4.22
Copy the contents of the board's layer and
paste it into a new channel.

16. Choose Filter, Render, Lighting
    Effects, using the Alpha 1 chan-
    nel as a displacement map. (See
    Figure 4.23.)

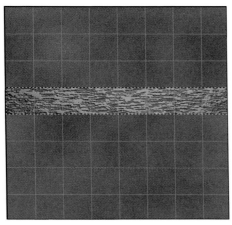

Filter: Render, Lighting Effects
Light Type: Spotlight, encompassing the entire board, from the top right
Intensity: 35
Focus: 69
Gloss: 0
Material: 69
Exposure: 0
Ambience: 8
Texture Channel: Alpha 1
Height: 50

Figure 4.23
Render the board's layer with the Lighting Effects filter, using the Alpha 1 channel as a displacement map.

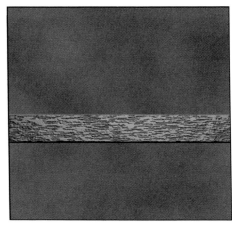

Style: Bevel and Emboss
Style: Outer Bevel
Technique: Chisel Hard
Depth: 1000%
Direction: Up
Size: 2
Soften: 0
Shading Angle: 90 degrees
Highlight Mode: Dark Yellow (hex# 51451F)

Figure 4.24
Apply an outer bevel to the board's layer.

17. To give the board a bit of depth, apply an outer bevel style to it by double-clicking the board's layer to bring up the Styles screen and applying the outer-bevel style with the settings listed alongside Figure 4.24.

18. Move this board up to the top edge and repeat steps 9–17 to create other boards, filling the image vertically. (Make sure you begin each board by taking a sample from the background layer.) Figure 4.25 shows my first layer of wood slats.

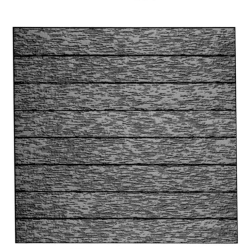

Figure 4.25
Repeat steps 9–17 to make different boards, and position them next to each other.

19. Now it's time to build the rest of the box panel. To begin, link all the layers except for one board layer—including the background layer—and press Ctrl+E to merge them. You should end up with one isolated board on its own layer, and the rest of the boards on the background layer.

20. The top board will still have its outer bevel style active, which should be flattened. Do this by creating a new layer, linking the

new layer with the board's layer, and merging the two.

21. You should now have a background layer with all the boards, minus one on its own layer. Make a copy of this board's layer.

22. With the copied layer active, choose Edit, Transform, Rotate 90 Degrees CCW. Move the rotated board to one side. (See Figure 4.26.)

23. Make both boards meet at a 45-degree angle. To do so, use the Polygonal Lasso tool to draw a selection that slices the tip off of each board at 45 degrees where they meet. This creates a stereotypical wooden-frame look. (See Figure 4.27.)

24. Merge the two board layers and make a copy of this new layer.

25. Rotate the copy 180 degrees so that you complete the frame, as shown in Figure 4.28. (You might have to chop off another end or two at 45-degree angles to make the frame look right.)

26. You should now have two layers on top of the background layer, each containing two boards joined at an angle; merge those two layers now.

27. To add a cross-bracing board diagonally between the frame, begin by using the Rectangular Marquee tool to select one of the boards in the background layer, and then press Ctrl+C to copy it.

28. Paste the copied board into the image. Then choose Edit, Transform, Rotate, and rotate and move it into place.

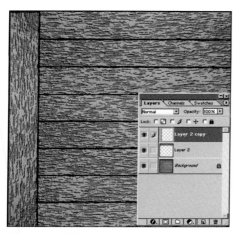

Figure 4.26
Copy the layer with the single board on it and rotate it 90 degrees. Move it to one side.

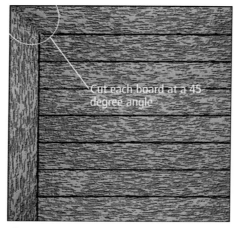

Figure 4.27
Slice the ends of each board where they meet at 45-degree angles.

Figure 4.28
Merge the two board layers, make a copy of the new layer, and rotate it 180 degrees.

29. Hack off the ends of the copied selection using the Polygonal Lasso tool.

30. When you're satisfied, merge that layer with the frame's layer; at this point, you should have only the background layer and the frame above it. (See Figure 4.29.)

31. Add a drop shadow to the frame's layer. This gives the frame excellent depth in contrast to the background layer's boards.

32. Flatten the entire image.

33. The boards are way too saturated with color; fix this by choosing Image, Adjust, Hue/Saturation, and sliding the Saturation slider down until the wood looks more dull and worn. (See Figure 4.30.)

34. Use the Burn tool with a low setting (such as 5 percent) and, with a large brush, burn in shadows all over the wood.

35. Add some large screws to the ends of all the visible, whole boards. (See the section "Rivets and Screws" in Chapter 2 for details on making 3D screws.) The ones I made here are simple, featuring a single flathead slot, and a darker shade to make them appear a bit rusty. (See Figure 4.31.)

36. Last, add some painted text to the outside board using the Text tool. I used the Spatter filter to break up the edges of

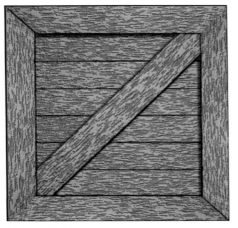

Figure 4.29
Create a cross-bracing board by making a copy of one of the boards in the background layer, rotating and positioning it, and hacking off the ends at 45-degree angles.

Figure 4.30
Apply a drop shadow to the frame, and then desaturate it.

Figure 4.31
Add screws to the edges of the whole boards for added realism.

the text, causing the paint to appear chipped. (See Figure 4.32.)

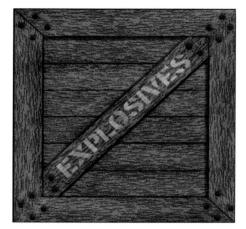

Figure 4.32
Finish the crate with some painted text.

As I said, normally I wouldn't make the wood from scratch like this; I just wanted to show you how many materials you can reproduce using Photoshop's filters. In the next section, I'll quickly make a wood crate using a photo of wood boards.

Munitions Crates with Canvas Cover

I'm going to speed this one up since you probably already have a solid

grasp of creating these crates. To follow along with this example, open the woodpic.jpg file located on the CD-ROM. This is an image of an old, wood shipping crate, the boards of which we'll extract to create the munitions crates. (See Figure 4.33.)

1. Start a new 512 × 512-pixel image with a black background. Use the Rectangular Marquee tool (or Polygonal Lasso tool) to select single boards from the woodpic.jpg image, copy them, and paste them into the new image. In Figure 4.34, I've

Figure 4.33
The woodpic.jpg file was used to create the munitions crates in this example.

created nine rows of them, adjusted the colors a bit, and applied a slight Inner Bevel style to make the boards a bit more 3D.

2. Complete the face of one crate by adding more boards around the border and across the middle, as I have done in Figure 4.35. The top boards can be on their own layer. Then apply an Inner Bevel and Drop Shadow style to this top layer, effectively raising the boards away from the background panel.

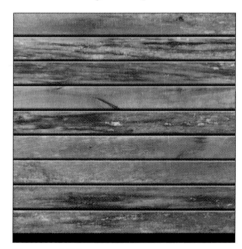

Figure 4.34
Select boards from the woodpic.jpg file and paste them into a new 512 × 512-pixel image.

Figure 4.35
Add a border of boards around and through the middle to complete the crate. Note the Drop Shadow style applied to the top boards to help raise them from the back panel.

Figure 4.36
Making a couple different crates by adding or removing boards helps to create a variety of crates for the next example.

3. Make a variant of the same crate, this time without top boards going through the middle. In Figure 4.36, I also added some stencil text to one crate. Finally, slightly desaturate the textures to give the crates a worn-in look.

Now that you have a couple of different crate textures, let's move on to creating the camouflage that you can use as a tie-down canvas for a stack of crates.

Camouflage

There must be dozens of different schemes for this type of material, from jungle to desert to what appears to be camouflage meant for the arctic tundra. None of those are difficult to make; it's just a matter of getting the four to ten colors recorded and applying them to foliage-like patterns. In this tutorial, you'll do regular Army camos. The trick to doing camouflage is alternating the layering properly.

1. Start a new 512 × 512-pixel RGB color image.

2. Fill the image using the Clouds filter, with your foreground set to a dark green, such as hex# 081406, and the background set to a more grayish dark green, such as hex# 192517.

3. Using the Channels palette, start a new channel.

4. Using the Lasso tool, create a goofy, foliage-like pattern that appears random—like an amoeba or something—as I have done in Figure 4.37. Fill this selection with pure white.

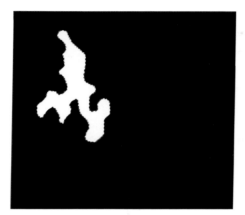

Figure 4.37
In a new channel, draw a foliage-like shape using one of the Lasso tools.

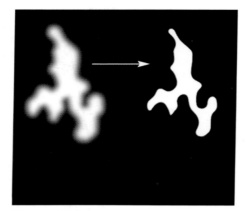

Figure 4.38
Apply the Gaussian Blur filter to the shape, and then resharpen it using the Levels command.

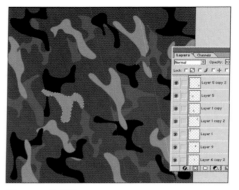

Figure 4.39
Fill the selections of the different shapes you created with dark tan, dark orange-brown, and black, in different arrangements and on separate layers.

5. Press Ctrl+D to deselect.

6. Choose Filter, Blur, Gaussian Blur, with a radius of about 5.0 pixels.

7. Choose Image, Adjust, Levels, and slide the Shadows and Highlights markers toward each other until the shape in the channel becomes crisp and sharp. (See Figure 4.38.) Don't bring the markers completely together, or you'll get aliased edges.

8. Repeat steps 3–7 to make about nine more of these shapes— some small and others larger, but not too big. *Make sure each shape is on its own channel!* That way, you can call up the individual shapes and overlap them later. Also, make sure each of the shapes is unique compared to the rest.

9. Ctrl+click one of the shape's channels to load its selection.

10. In the Layers palette, start a new layer.

11. Fill the selection with a medium tan (hex# 737244), a dark orange-brown (hex# 3F250E), or pure black (hex# 000000).

12. Repeat steps 9–11 for each of the remaining shapes you created, and fill them with one of the three colors mentioned. Try to make things random, overlapping, but not too cluttered, as I have done in Figure 4.39. The trick to a nice camo is to even out the color scheme and to have the colored shapes interlayered nicely.

13. When you're satisfied with your camo, choose Layer, Flatten Image.

14. Choose Filter, Texture, Texturizer, and select the Canvas option. This gives the camo a perfect, rough style.

15. Adjust the levels to suit.

16. Choose Image, Adjust, Hue/ Saturation, and desaturate the colors a tad to wash them out appropriately. (See Figure 4.40.)

You can now scale down this pattern to something like 128 × 128 pixels and set it as a pattern for the next section.

Adding the Canvas Cover to a Crate Stack

Picking up from the previous crate creation example, let's finish the texture by making a 4 × 4 stack of wooden crates. In all, this texture can be wrapped around a large cube primitive in a game, making it appear as though there are eight crates together, tied down with a camouflage canvas.

1. Start a new 1024 × 1024-pixel image with a black background. Copy and paste your crate textures and arrange them so that they appear stacked, with a slight offset, as I have done in Figure 4.41. The top two crates can have a slight drop shadow to them as well.

2. In Figure 4.42, I've used the freehand Lasso tool to create a wavy selection across the crates and filled it with the camouflage pattern. Note that the bottom portion of each "wave" represents where a rope is running through a metal eyelet, holding down the canvas.

Filter: Texture, Texturizer
Texture: Canvas
Scaling: 50%
Relief: 2
Light Direction: Top

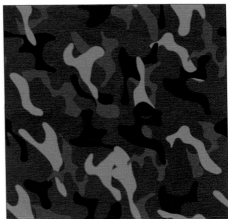

Figure 4.40
Flatten the image and apply the Canvas filter. Adjust the levels and saturation to suit.

Figure 4.41
Add four copies of the wooden crates you created earlier to a 1024 × 1024-pixel image.

Figure 4.42
Create a wavy selection across the crates and fill it with the camouflage texture.

Figure 4.43
Dodge and burn the camouflage to make the texture appear 3D- and material-like.

Figure 4.44
Add a Drop Shadow style to the canvas, some metal eyelets, and rope to complete the texture.

3. Use the Dodge and Burn tools to force the camouflage material to have a 3D appearance. Do this by gently dodging along the crest where each wave of the material exists, and burn between them. (See Figure 4.43.) This is a quick and effective way to create wrinkles in textures to simulate fabrics. Notice that the light areas (dodged) stand out, whereas the dark areas (burned) are recessed.

4. In Figure 4.44, I completed the texture by adding a Drop Shadow style to the camouflage and then some beveled eyelets and rope lines. The lines also have a drop shadow.

I think I've seen this texture in almost every First-Person Shooter (FPS) military game I've played. (See Figure 4.45.) Note that the top portion of the cube of crates is just the camouflage texture again, with dodged and

Figure 4.45
The completed canvas-covered crate texture wrapped around a cube primitive.

burned striations emanating from each corner.

RPG-7 Grenade Launcher

I'll wrap up this chapter with a cool example of skinning a 3D model. I've been modeling and animating for about seven years now, primarily using Caligari trueSpace and 3D Studio Max. trueSpace is by far one of the most powerful modeling programs I've ever used, mainly due to its excellent modeling interface. 3D Studio Max, despite the expensive price tag, is the foremost top-modeling and animation software in the gaming world, but the modeling interface is a bit more cumbersome. Maya is a close second that many artists prefer, although Max and Maya have nearly identical graphical prowess.

I can't go too deep into modeling here because this is a texturing book. (For full coverage on modeling, bones, skinning, and game export of 3D models, see my book titled *2D Artwork and 3D Modeling for Game Artists*, published by Premier Press. There, I cover every detail of creating

weapon and character models from start to finish for games.) However, for this example, I've modeled an RPG-7 (rocket-propelled grenade) launcher and grenade in trueSpace and neatly unwrapped their *U-V coordinates* in 3D Studio Max (with help from Right Hemisphere's DeepUV software). The launcher and grenade models and their meshes are displayed in Figure 4.46.

note

I've saved the RPG-7 model in different formats such as trueSpace, 3D Studio Max, LightWave, and DirectX. Look for them on the CD-ROM in the Chapter 4 folder along with the model's U-V maps and textures.

If you know anything about 3D models in general, you'll know that they consist of points (called *vertices*) that are interconnected by lines (called *edges*) that form a closed object. When a 3D model is initially created, it has no texture but contains an invisible set of duplicate vertices that represent the model's texture coordinates, or U-V coordinates. These coordinates dictate how the model's texture "wraps" around itself, which is commonly known as a *skin*. To properly paint a texture for a model, these coordinates must be unwrapped and laid flat on a texture map, much the way a t-shirt would lay flat if you cut it apart at the seams.

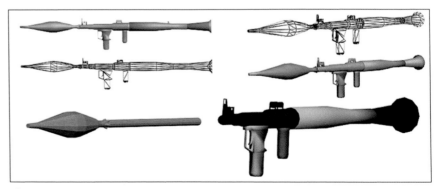

Figure 4.46
The RPG-7 grenade and launcher models that will be textured in this section.

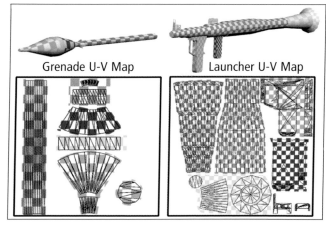

Figure 4.47
The RPG-7's texture map. Note the checkerboard colors on the map areas and how they correspond to the 3D models.

or bunched coordinates show up as skewed or distorted checkerboards on the 3D model. Use Figure 4.47 to refer to the areas of the map I'll be texturing as you follow along.

I'm using several photographs of rusty, worn metal to help generate the textures for the RPG, which are also located on the CD-ROM. You can follow this tutorial by opening the RPG's U-V maps as a starting point. I'm only going to generalize on the steps I took to create these textures because each step took a modest amount of manipulation to get the image to look right. However, most of what I do is usually just a matter of adjusting levels, curves, hue/saturation, brightness/contrast, and dodging/burning.

1. To create the base metal texture of the main barrel of the RPB (the part into which the grenade attaches), I used a close-up picture of the side of one of those Caterpillar

For the following example, I've unwrapped both the grenade and launcher and displayed their wireframe reference maps on two separate image files. (See `rpg7_grenade_uv.psd` and `rpg7_launcher_uv.psd` on the CD-ROM.) On top of the maps, I've filled the U-V areas with simple checkerboard textures of different colors to help direct you to the parts of the map that correlate to their respective parts on the 3D models. (See Figure 4.47.) This is a good pretexturing technique to practice; it will help you to determine if your U-V coordinates have been successfully unwrapped. Crossed

The Rocket-Propelled Grenade Launcher

I got the idea to model this weapon from the cover of the December 15, 2003 issue of Time Magazine. The cover shows an Iraqi sporting a weathered RPG-7B. (See the cover by visiting http://www.time.com/time/magazine/archive/ and clicking on the December 15 cover issue.)

The RPG-7 is an anti-tank grenade launcher and descendant of the World War II German Panzerfaust. It is a common, shoulder-mounted weapon among Middle-Eastern countries, weighing about 15 pounds and having an effective firing range of more than 1,000 meters. It is an inexpensive, single-shot weapon that's capable of penetrating vulnerable rear points of many military tanks, as well as being a devastating antipersonnel device. The Vietcong used the RPG-7 in the Vietnam War, and it was also used extensively in the Afghanistan war during the Soviet occupation. The RPG-7 can currently be found in use in more than 40 countries, including China, Iran, Iraq, Romania, and Pakistan. It is the weapon of choice for many infantrymen and guerillas around the world.

Figure 4.49
Copy a portion of the rusty panel picture and paste it over the main barrel section of the RPG's U-V map.

Figure 4.48
The `rustypanel2.jpg` file used to create the base metal texture for the main barrel of the RPG.

tractors. Open `rustypanel2.jpg` on the CD-ROM. (See Figure 4.48.)

2. Following the RPG's U-V map (see `rpg7_grenade_launcher.psd` on the CD-ROM), I copied a section of the rusty panel picture and pasted it into place over the main barrel section. (See Figure 4.49.)

3. Then I desaturated this portion, making it much more gray. After that, on a separate layer, I filled the same selection with a white-to-black reflected gradient. (See Figure 4.50.) The

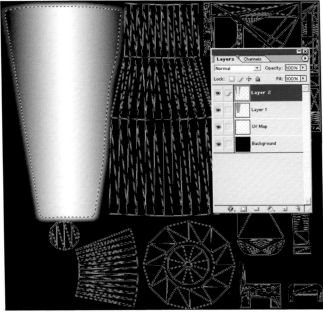

gradient will be used to make the texture appear rounded.

4. The reflected gradient layer's blending mode is changed to Overlay. After merging this layer down to the rusty metal layer, I dodged the center to enhance the shininess and burned the edges to fade it off.

Figure 4.50
Here, I desaturated the metal texture and placed a reflected gradient on top of it. This will be used to make the texture appear rounded.

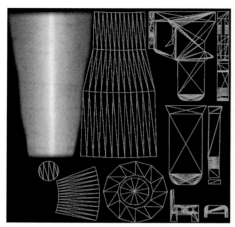

Figure 4.51
The gradient layer is changed to Overlay and then merged down. Dodging the center enhances the shininess.

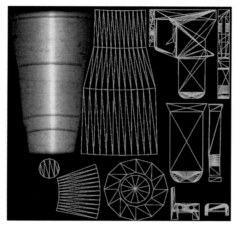

Figure 4.52
The final barrel texture is changed to a dark gold, and shadowed segments are added.

Figure 4.53
The woodpic2.jpg photo, used to create the rear portion of the RPG.

The entire area was then adjusted for overall saturation, hue, and brightness. (See Figure 4.51.)

5. I changed the barrel's color to a deep gold by clicking the Variations command and selecting a more yellow color. To make the shadowed segments seen in Figure 4.52, I merely copied portions of the barrel texture onto their own layers and applied drop shadow styles to them. The steps taken up until now constitute 90 percent of the techniques I use to create metal-based textures from photos.

6. The rear portion of the RPG is typically made of bound, thin strips of wood. This is the shoulder rest area; it protects the shoulder from the heat of the rocket. (Wood is a poor heat conductor, whereas metal allows heat to flow through it as if the metal weren't even there). I'll use a photograph of a wooden fence for this part. Open the woodpic2.jpg image located on the CD-ROM, shown in Figure 4.53.

7. The rear portion of the RGP's U-V map is right next to the front barrel. In Figure 4.54, I've made a selection from the wood picture and pasted it onto the photo. Because the U-V map is "relaxed"—that is, the coordinates are laid out in a natural position to prevent distortion of the texture—you'll notice that the U-V area for the rear is V-shaped. Therefore, I've scaled the texture and clicked Edit, Transform, Distort to distort the texture to conform to the U-V's shape.

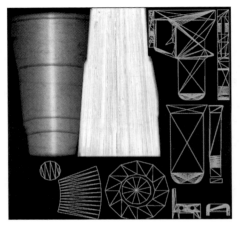

Figure 4.54
A portion of the wood picture is copied and placed on the U-V map. The top end (which represents the back of the barrel) is distorted to fit naturally on the map.

8. In Figure 4.55, I've darkened (via Levels and Curves) the wood, dodged and burned it, and added metal straps where the transitions of the barrel occur. This completes this portion of the barrel.

9. If you happened to look to the *Time Magazine* Web site and viewed the December 15, 2003 cover, the RPG pictured there has a distinctive scratchy, bright metal texture for the weapon's trigger point. To simulate this,

Figure 4.55
The rear barrel texture is darkened and metal straps are added. The straps on a real RPG hold all the wood slats in place on the metal barrel.

I've taken a picture of the side of some disgusting old trash dumpster, to which I'll extract a texture. You can find the file called rustypanel3.jpg on the CD-ROM. (See Figure 4.56.)

10. In Figure 4.57, I've copied a portion of the dumpster image onto the trigger area's U-V map.

11. Just as I did earlier with the main barrel of the RPG, I desaturated the texture and then added a gradient on top of it for use in creating some form

Figure 4.56
The rustypanel3.jpg file used to create the texture for the trigger point of the RPG.

Figure 4.57
Here a portion of the dumpster panel is copied onto the trigger's U-V map.

of highlighting and shadowing. In Figure 4.58, the gradient is instead Linear, but it could be anything else, such as black-and-white Clouds or Noise filters.

Figure 4.58
The texture is then desaturated and a linear gradient is applied on top of it.

Figure 4.59
The gradient is changed to Overlay. Rivets are added, along with thin wood slats for the grips like when I created the rear portion of the RPG's barrel.

Figure 4.60
The rest of the U-V components are filled in the same way as the main barrel, which completes the texture.

12. The gradient's layer is changed to Overlay. In Figure 4.59, I've adjusted the overall brightness and saturation and added some rivets. The handle of the trigger area and rear handle are made of wood slats as well, so I made them like I did the rear barrel and adjusted the colors. Along with the usual dodging and burning, I added a drop shadow from the metal portions to make them appear raised.

13. As you can see, things are just repetitive now. The exhaust portion of the RPG is filled in exactly as I did the main barrel, and with a few more adjustments here and there, the texture is complete. (See Figure 4.60.)

Granted, if I were to explain everything I did during each step of this texturing process, I would fill 100 pages! Much of it is just small adjustments until it looks right, or walking away and coming back after a while to notice what other changes should be made. The RPG's grenade was textured in the same way as the rest. Figure 4.61 shows both textures and the completed RPG-7 weapon rendered in 3D Studio Max.

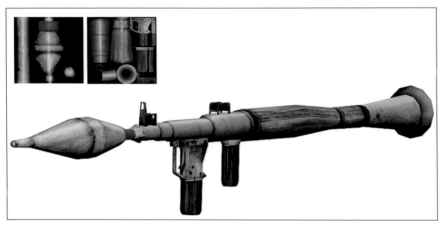

Figure 4.61
The final grenade and launcher textures applied to the RPG-7 and rendered in 3D Studio Max.

metal or wooden base. As I've shown you, you can create these textures from scratch using only a few of Photoshop's default filters, or you can use the more preferred method of using photographs of real-world items. From panels to crates to model skins, these textures easily found their way into a military scheme, but you could apply them to anything else in the gaming world.

Two notes about this model: I created a separate model and texture for the grenade. That's because in a 3D game, the grenade would launch away from the gunner and would have to be a separate model and texture. Also, if your model is built and textured in a program such as 3D Studio Max or Maya, most likely it can work in most 3D game engines. Game developers generally make plug-ins to export your models from these programs to fit in their game engines; it's usually a matter of optimizing the model and saving the texture in the appropriate file format. The model demonstrated here, without the grenade, averaged about 1,250 polygons (which is high for a weapon model); however, after applying a MultiRes modifier in Max, I can get a level of detail of about 650 polygons without a noticeable change.

Summary

This chapter presented a handful of the most common textures found in video games—namely, textures with a

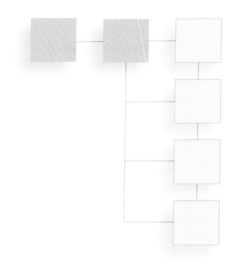

CHAPTER 5

Slums

Volenti non fit iniuria…

Injury is not done to a willing person…

Poverty is an unfortunate consequence of the human race. It exists in all countries in the world—some much more than others—and I truly wish no being should ever have to live in such a degrading environment. However, this state of texturing is much more challenging and useful in many video games. You could also group the textures presented here with the previous chapter, "Military Textures." In this chapter, I will show you the following:

- How to create a seamlessly tileable brick wall by extracting a single pattern from an existing brick wall photograph

- How to use the base brick pattern, in conjunction with a photograph of a wood crate texture, to create a slum wall, complete with a bashed-in area and graffiti

- How to create rusty metal from scratch in Photoshop

- How to use a photograph of a rusty panel to create a tileable rust pattern

- How to use the rust pattern to create an old oil drum texture, with a gouge in the middle of it

- How to apply the completed texture on the 3D drum model's U-V map and display it in a video game in conjunction with the fire sprite animation performed in Chapter 3, "Sprites"

note

Look at the texture photographs I've provided you on the CD-ROM. There's a set of images I took of the walls from a 200-year-old demolished building that would be perfect for both this chapter and Chapter 4.

Brick Walls

Again, the best way to develop a good brick wall texture is by photograph. However, rather than taking a picture of an entire wall and trying to make it seamlessly tileable on all sides, it's sometimes better to extract a single brick pattern, clean it up, and then fill a 512 × 512-pixel image with it. Here I'll demonstrate this technique and then use it as a base to create a slum wall.

Basic Brick Wall

For this tutorial, I took a picture of a brick portion of the side of my house. This image will serve as the basis with which to create a seamless brick wall.

1. In Photoshop, open the `brickwall.jpg` file on the CD-ROM. (See Figure 5.1.)

Figure 5.1
Open the `brickwall.jpg` image on the CD-ROM.

2. Notice that the image is tilted slightly clockwise by about 1 degree. To fix this, click Image, Rotate Canvas, Arbitrary. Then type 1 in the Angle field, select CCW (counterclockwise), and click OK. The bricks (not the canvas) should be somewhat level now. (See Figure 5.2.)

Figure 5.2
Straighten out the image using the Rotate Canvas feature.

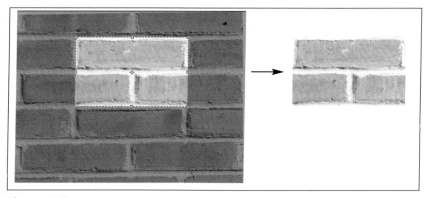

Figure 5.3
Use the Crop tool to isolate a tileable pattern from the brick wall.

3. Using the Crop tool, select an area in the image that includes a single brick on top with two half bricks beneath, like the pattern you created in the preceding section. Remember to include one-half of the mortar that surrounds these bricks so that when the pattern is tiled, the halves will constitute a whole. (See Figure 5.3.)

4. Click Edit, Define Pattern, give the pattern a name, and click OK.

5. Create a new 1024 × 1024-pixel RGB image with a transparent background.

6. Click Edit, Fill.

7. Under Contents, select Pattern. In the Custom Pattern list, select your new brick pattern, and click OK. You should now have a filled image similar to the one in Figure 5.4.

Figure 5.4
Define your brick selection as a pattern and fill a blank image with it.

8. In my filled image, I see a handful of imperfections that repeat all over the place. (See Figure 5.5.) To eliminate these flaws in your image, return to the first image from which you created the pattern, and use the Clone Stamp or Healing Brush tool to cover the blemishes. In addition, you can use the Clone Stamp tool to eliminate the shadows on the mortar. (Copy over shadowed areas with non-shadowed mortar.) Alternatively, you can use the Dodge tool with a low exposure setting to do the trick.

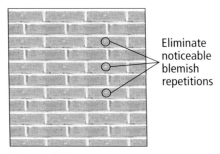

Figure 5.5
Find any repeating blemishes on your pattern and get rid of them by using the Clone Stamp tool. Dodge out noticeable shadows as well.

9. As you make adjustments and clean up your pattern, redefine the pattern and fill your test image with it to see your progress. (See Figure 5.6.)

Of course, the more time you spend cleaning up the texture, the better it will look. (Then again, you'll only be dirtying it up in the next section). The main point is that you want to eliminate any noticeable, repeating blemishes. That said, don't go overboard. Just make sure nothing stands out. Here are some things to keep in mind when creating tiling textures like this:

■ Use the Clone Stamp tool avidly to copy good areas and paste them over bad ones.

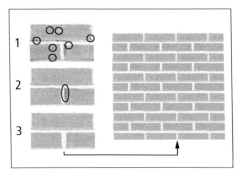

Figure 5.6
Keep cleaning up your pattern until it's nice and even. Fill the pattern on an image to make sure it looks good.

■ Use the Clone Stamp tool to even out the texture.

■ Dodge (and burn) shadows and highlights out of (or into) the image.

■ Zoom in on your work to aid in detailed operations.

■ Take your time. This is a small piece of work to make a huge wall!

Slum Wall Example

Here, I'm going to take the cleaned-up break pattern from before and use it as the basis to create a dirty, broken brick wall. If you'd like to try following along, use the woodpic.jpg and

brickwall2.jpg files on the CD-ROM as a basis for creating the entire image. See Figures 5.7 through 5.14 for the steps I took in creating this wall.

Figure 5.7
This is woodpic.jpg, which is a picture of a weathered wooden crate. I used the Polygonal Lasso tool to select and copy only the wood from this image.

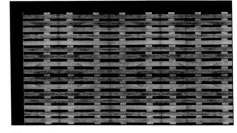

Figure 5.8
In a new 1204 × 512-pixel image filled with black, I pasted several copies of the wood crate on a new layer. This will serve as the wood wall frame behind the brick wall.

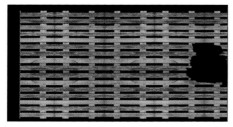

Figure 5.9
Here, I used the Lasso tool to select a jagged area on the right side of the wood, and I deleted it. This will be where the brick wall will appear bashed open.

Figure 5.10
To the wood layer, I applied an Outer Bevel style, using a Cove-Shallow contour within that style's options. To chop up the bevel, I applied a brick texture, also within the style's options.

Figure 5.11
On a new layer, I filled it with the basic brick texture from the previous tutorial.

Figure 5.12
Here, I adjusted the levels to darken the brick, and I adjusted the hue/saturation.

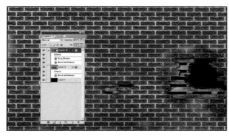

Figure 5.13
I used the Lasso tool to select a huge hole and another smaller one, and I deleted the brick selections, exposing the wood behind the wall. I also applied the same Outer Bevel to the wall as with the wood layer. Finally, I touched up the brick all over with the Burn tool to dirty it up.

Figure 5.14
Finally, I added a few blast marks from the tutorial in Chapter 2, "Nasty Decals," and some graffiti.

In Figure 5.14, the graffiti was just some scaled, modified text that I manipulated in a new channel and then applied a colored gradient to. I applied the Lighting Effects filter using a copy of the brick wall in a new channel as a displacement map, giving it the impression of paint being sprayed on top of brick. The whole thing was then dodged, burned, and desaturated to complete the effect.

Rusty Metal

There are a number of ways to generate rust from scratch in Photoshop; I prefer to use a photograph of a nice rusty panel. (See rustypanel.jpg on the CD-ROM.) However, here's a quick way to make workable rust:

Figure 5.15
Fill a new image with the Clouds filter using rusty brown-orange colors.

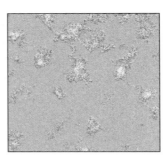

Filter: Sketch, **Notepaper Image Balance:** 25 **Graininess:** 10 **Relief:** 10

Figure 5.16
In a new channel, apply the Clouds, Difference Clouds, Noise, and Notepaper filters.

Figure 5.17
Copy the channel and paste it into a new layer. Change the layer's blending mode to Color Burn to complete the effect.

1. Start a new 1024 × 1024-pixel RGB image with a transparent background. Fill it with the Clouds filter, using rusty brown-orange colors such as hex# 533301 and hex# 8F4103. (See Figure 5.15.)

2. Go to the Channels palette and start a new channel. Apply the Clouds filter. Then apply the Difference Clouds filter a few times.

3. Apply Filter, Noise, Add Noise—about 12 percent.

4. Apply Filter, Sketch, Notepaper. Your new channel should look like mine in Figure 5.16.

5. Press Ctrl+A to select the entire contents of this channel.

6. Go back to the Layers palette, and then press Ctrl+V to paste the channel's image into a new layer.

7. Change this new layer's blending mode to Color Burn. (See Figure 5.17.) Now you have some decent, workable rust.

Rusty Oil Drum

The base texture for this example uses a picture I took of a rusty metal panel. Then we'll apply some ribs and a small gouge.

1. Open the `rustypanel.jpg` image located on the CD-ROM. Click on the Rectangular Marquee tool and set the tool's style at the top to Fixed Size, with a width and height of 512 pixels. Click once on the image and select a consistent rusty area on the image, such as in Figure 5.18.

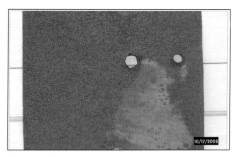

Figure 5.18
Make a 512 × 512 pixel selection in the
rustypanel.jpg file.

2. Press Ctrl+C to copy this selection, and close the file. Start a new 512 × 512-pixel image, and press Ctrl+V to paste this selection into it.

3. This type of base texture is excellent for use with Photoshop's Pattern Maker filter. That's because the texture is consistent throughout the image. Click Filter, Pattern Maker (Ctrl+Alt+Shift+X). In this filter, select the entire image. Then on the right side of the screen, click the Use Image Size button. Click Generate. It won't look like much happened, but each time you click Generate, a new seamlessly tileable image is randomly generated. When you're satisfied, click OK.

Figure 5.19
Use the selection to generate a small rust pattern, and use it to fill a 512 × 512-pixel image.

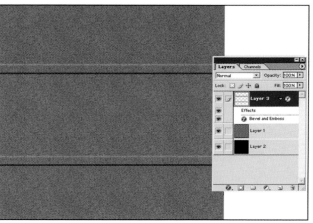

Figure 5.20
Make two rectangular selections across the texture and copy them to a new layer. Apply an Inner Bevel style to them to make them 3D.

4. Click Image, Image Size, and change the image to 128 × 128 pixels.

5. Click Edit, Define Pattern. Make this a rust pattern you can use to fill other images.

6. Close the file. Start a new 512 × 512 image and fill it with the rust pattern. (See Figure 5.19.) Now you have a nice base rust texture with which to work.

7. Use the Rectangular Marquee tool to make two thin selections across the image. Right-click on the selections and choose Layer Via Copy. This will be the oil drum's ribs.

8. To this new layer, add Inner Bevel style. Figure 5.20 shows my bevel; notice that the Highlight mode of the bevel is a deep orange.

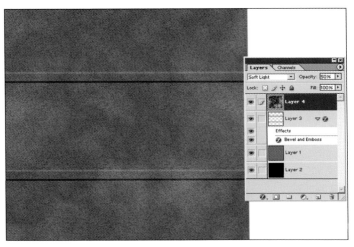

Figure 5.21
Dirty up the texture with the Burn tool or a cloudy layer set to Soft Light.

Figure 5.22
To make a tear in the metal, start with a thin selection.

9. You can apply the Burn tool to dirty up the drum, or do like I did in Figure 5.21. I created another layer on top of all layers; then I applied the Clouds and Difference Clouds filters. After that, I set this layer's blending mode to Soft Light.

10. Let's add a tear in the metal. Use the Lasso Marquee tool to make a thin, tear-looking selection. (See Figure 5.22.)

11. Start a new layer above the base rust layer.

12. With the selection still active, fill this selection with pure black.

13. Apply a downward Inner Bevel style to this tear. In Figure 5.23, I also applied a Contour option in the bevel panel.

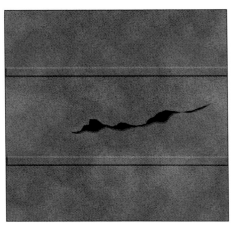

Figure 5.23
Fill the selection with black on a new layer above the rust layer. Add a downward Inner Bevel style to complete the effect.

14. As I demonstrated in Chapter 2, in the "Peeling Paint on Metal" section, dodge the tips of some of the curved areas, and burn behind them to make the torn metal appear to be curved both in and out. (See Figure 5.24.)

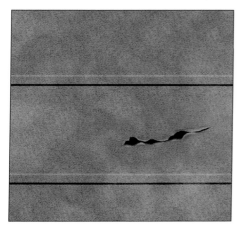

Figure 5.24
Dodge and burn the edges of the tear to give it the illusion of being curved in and out.

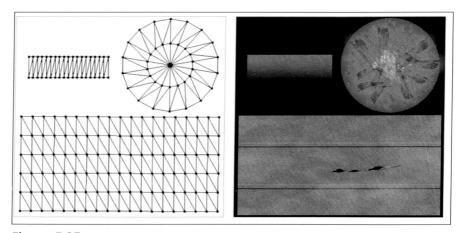

Figure 5.25
The U-V map of a wood burning oil drum.

Oil Drum U-V Map

The texture in the previous example would be placed into action around a 3D object in the shape of a cylinder. Just like the crate examples in Chapter 4, the oil drum model would be a simple cylinder whose U-V coordinates were laid flat on a map. The map, shown in Figure 5.25, contains the rectangular outside surface of the drum, followed by the top and bottom circular end pieces. I decide, however, to make the top piece concave in shape, and on the map I place a glowing ember texture to be the base of some wood-burning fire.

Figure 5.26
The completed drum texture, including the fire sprite animation presented in Chapter 3.

In Figure 5.26, I've wrapped the skin around the oil drum model I made in trueSpace, and on top placed the fire sprite animation I did in Chapter 3.

Summary

Wall textures, as with most other textures, begin their lives with some sort of base, seamlessly tileable pattern with which to build the rest of the texture. In this chapter, I demonstrated how to use a photograph of a brick wall, extract a single brick pattern from it, and use it to create an entire brick texture that is tileable with itself. This base texture was used in conjunction with an image of wood to create a decent-looking slum wall.

The nature of this type of environment also allows for rusty metal objects such as oil drums and dumpsters. By using a base photograph of a rusty panel, I showed how to extract a tileable pattern and use it to create a cool wood-burning oil drum that utilized the fire sprite animation from Chapter 3. Applying such a texture to a 3D model is just like the crate example from Chapter 4—using a 3D modeling program to model and unwrap the U-V texture coordinates to create a U-V map, which you can use as a reference to complete the model's texture.

CHAPTER 6

MEDIEVAL/FANTASY TEXTURES

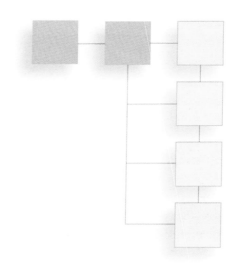

Draconis: Alatus durus corpus; manibus pedibusque…

The dragon: Harsh body with wings; hands and feet, tooth and nail…

If you've played *Return to Castle Wolfenstein*, you might have noticed that many of the textures present in that game are stone based. The game has rustic medieval castle embattlements, ramparts carved from granite or limestone, cement-formed gargoyles, keystones, and archways. I'll cover several ways to create some of these walls and doors, including some fantasy items such as dragon eyes, teeth, and skin. In this chapter, you'll learn how to create the following:

- Medieval stone walls and floors that are appropriate for castles
- A stone wall transition set
- Wall with a cement gargoyle image
- A wrought-iron castle door
- Dragon eyes, teeth, and skin
- Fiery text, for use as console and cover art
- A wizard's glass orb

Stone Walls/Floors

You can apply these tutorials to walls, floors, or both. The next example demonstrates the more popular way of creating this type of texture: through the use of digital photographs of real stone walls.

Medieval Castle Stone Wall, Using Photos

This tutorial shows how to use a digital photograph of an object that will represent the base texture of the final texture image. In this case, I've taken a picture of the side of a 200-year-old German mill that is near me in New Jersey. There were a lot of German settlers in my area in the 1800s, so many of the now-preserved buildings were made from stones that varied in size.

1. To follow along, open the `stonewallpic1.jpg` image located on the CD-ROM. This image is larger than 512 × 512 pixels, so it has enough area to crop out ample texture information for our needs.

tip

When you're acquiring digital images for texture composites, it's best to get full sunlight shots, particularly in mid-morning or late afternoon when the sun's rays can hit the objects straight on, or perpendicularly. Sunlight is one of the best light sources for illuminating your props because it contains the full spectrum of colors and then some. Try to avoid getting shadows in your image because they relay improper depth cueing when they're composited with the rest of your texture.

2. Select the Rectangular Marquee tool. In this tool's top options, under Style, choose Fixed Size. Then enter `512` pixels for both the Width and Height parameters. Click once in the image, which creates a perfect 512 × 512 marquee selection. In Figure 6.1, I chose the bottom-right corner of the image, which seemed to represent a selection of rocks that had the most lighting consistency.

Figure 6.1
Open the `stonewallpic1.jpg` file and make a 512 × 512-pixel selection of stones.

Figure 6.2
Copy and paste the selection to a new file. Desaturate the image so that it's not so vivid.

Filter: Other, Offset
Horizontal: 256 pixels
Vertical: 256 pixels
Undefined Areas: wrap around

Figure 6.3
Offset the image one-half of the length and width to make it seamlessly tileable.

Figure 6.4
Use the Healing Brush tool to get rid of the seams in the middle of the image.

3. With the selection still active, press Ctrl+C to copy it. Then click File, New, and the parameters of the new file creation are set automatically to 512 × 512 pixels, representing the copied selection stored in the buffer. Click OK to create a new image, and press Ctrl+V to paste the selection into the new image. You now have a perfect 512 × 512-pixel base texture with which to work.

4. The colors in this image are way too bright; most games look better with desaturated images. Choose Image, Adjustments, Hue/Saturation, and slide the Saturation marker to the left until you've washed out much of the color information, as I have in Figure 6.2.

5. The image needs to be seamlessly tileable so that it can fill large walls. Click Filter, Other, Offset, and enter 256 pixels, or one-half the length and width of the image for both Horizontal and Vertical wraparound. This makes the image shift right and down, creating a seamlessly tileable image. (See Figure 6.3.) We need to fix the image internally so that it looks normal again.

6. To fix the seams inside of the image, I recommend using the Healing Brush tool. (Press J.) This tool looks like a band-aid on the toolbar. Some people prefer to use the Clone Stamp tool to clone stones from one portion of the image and paste over the seams, but the Healing Brush tool cleverly blends color information from one area to the other, eliminating the common smearing effect typically resulting from the Clone Stamp tool. In Figure 6.4, I've brushed the stones near the seams directly onto the seams. Try to work a bit diligently here to get a decent image, and try not to brush onto the outer edges of the image; that's where the image maintains its seamless tiling information.

7. Now let's use this base pattern to fill a texture panel. The texture at this size would be out of proportion in a video game; the stones are too large. Click Image, Image Size, and change the image to 256 × 256 pixels. Then make it a stored pattern in Photoshop by clicking Edit, Define Pattern. This stores the image as a pattern in the pattern list.

8. Close the image and save it if you want. Start a new 512 × 512-pixel, RGB color image with a transparent background. Then fill this image with the pattern you just made by clicking Edit, Fill, and select the stone wall pattern from the Custom Pattern list. Four tiles of this pattern are placed in the image. (See Figure 6.5.)

9. Notice in Figure 6.5 that I've circled areas that display noticeable stone repetitions. Again, use the Healing Brush tool to get rid of as many of these items in the image that stand out. By doing this, the player won't notice that the tiling texture repeats itself over and over on a wall. Figure 6.6 shows my final texture. There are still a few stones that repeat in the image, but they aren't as noticeable as the ones I got rid of.

Figure 6.7 shows the complete texture tiled on a castle wall model. This texture would work well on a castle wall in *Return to Castle Wolfenstein*. A single texture of this nature is used on nearly 80 percent of the castle in the game and can barely be noticed as just one texture.

Blending Objects

Many times, a texture artist takes an existing texture and adds objects to it for use in other areas of a building to break up a monotonous pattern. Try this: Open the `stonewallpic2.jpg` image on the CD-ROM. This is a picture of a wooden window on the side of the same old mill whose wall helped us create the previous texture. (See Figure 6.8.)

You can copy the window from this image using the Lasso Marquee tool. I set this tool's options to Feather, 5 pixels, and then I freehand selected the window. After copying the window, I pasted it back into the final texture from the previous example, scaled it, and desaturated it. The feathering helps it to blend into the image better. (See Figure 6.9.) You might also have to gently erase

Figure 6.5
Reduce the image to 256 × 256 pixels and create a stored pattern out of it. Fill a new 512 × 512 image with this pattern.

Figure 6.6
Use the Healing Brush tool to get rid of any noticeable, repeating stones in the image.

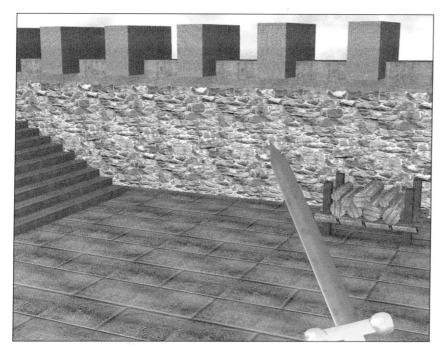

Figure 6.7
The completed texture tiled on a castle wall model.

Figure 6.8
The stonewallpic2.jpg image. This is a picture of a wooden window taken from the same old mill building that was used in the previous example.

Figure 6.9
Copy the window using the Lasso Marquee tool with a slight feather. Paste it into the previous texture example, scale it, and desaturate it.

around the window's edges to get it to blend in better.

Now you have another texture tile that you can use to break up a wall pattern made with the previous example.

Applying Snow

The castle in *Return to Castle Wolfenstein* is located somewhere in the Alps, so many of the objects in it are dusted with snow. You can add snow to the texture you created in Figure 6.6 like this: Select the Magic Wand tool and uncheck Contiguous in the tool's options. Then click on

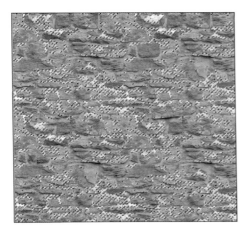

Figure 6.10
Use the Magic Wand tool to select most of the mortar in the Medieval Castle wall texture, in one click.

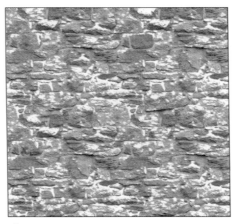

Figure 6.11
Fill the selection with the Clouds filter, using off-white colors to complete the snow effect.

In Figure 6.12, I tiled this snowy stone texture on a medieval building that has a wintery surrounding, which makes it blend in perfectly.

Stone Wall Transition Set

Keeping with the original medieval stone wall texture, I'll show you how to make a quick transition set to help better break up repeating patterns. In Chapter 1, "Texturing Basics," I mentioned how some game engines can utilize texture sets—small groups of similar textures that the game engine can randomly tile on brush surfaces, thereby breaking up monotonous texture repetition.

any white-ish area on the image, where the mortar exists between the stones. Doing so selects most white-ish areas in the image, primarily where the mortar exists. (See Figure 6.10.)

With the selection still active, set the foreground and background colors to an off-white, such as hex# EFEFEF and hex#D6D6D6. Click Filter, Render, Clouds, and the stones in your image become dusted with snow. (See Figure 6.11.)

The best way to create a set is to have several base photographs of different areas of the same type of image. If you open the stonewallpic3.jpg image on the CD-ROM, you'll see that it is a picture I took of the old mill wall, right next to the area I took from stonewallpic1.jpg.

Figure 6.12
The completed snowy stone wall texture in a game.

These two images aren't identical; rather, they are a continuum of different portions of the same wall.

To make a transition set, first open the original medieval stone wall texture (or open stonewall2.jpg on the CD-ROM). Because this is the final, game-ready tiling texture, we'll need its edges to be the *master* tiling pattern so that all other textures can tile with it. Select the Rectangular Marquee tool, and in the tool's options at the top, set the Style to Fixed Size. Set the selection size to 480 × 480 pixels, and set a Feather value of 20 pixels. Click in the image, and move the selection so that it's in the center of the image. (See Figure 6.13.)

The feathering of the selection causes the corners of the marquee to be rounded and feathers everything so that it blends easily with another stone background image without harsh seams. With the selection still active, press D on your keyboard to reset the Color Control Panel, and then press Delete to kill the selection, leaving you with a feathered stone border. (See Figure 6.14.) This border is what we want. It contains the seamless tiling information.

Repeat steps 1–9 of the earlier section "Medieval Castle Stone Wall, Using Photos," but this time use the stonewallpic3.jpg image instead. When you're finished, you should have another texture that's similar to the original texture you made. However, this new texture's borders are not tileable with the original. Copy the feathered border you made in Figure 6.14, and paste it on top of your completed texture. This makes your new texture seamlessly tileable with the original. (See Figure 6.15.)

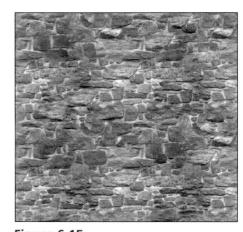

Figure 6.15
Create a new stone wall texture using the stonewallpic3.jpg image. Paste the feathered selection on top of this, making this new texture seamlessly tileable with the original stone wall texture.

Figure 6.13
Create a 480 × 480-pixel selection with a 20-pixel feather in the center of the medieval stone wall texture.

Figure 6.14
Delete the selection, leaving a feathered, seamlessly tileable border.

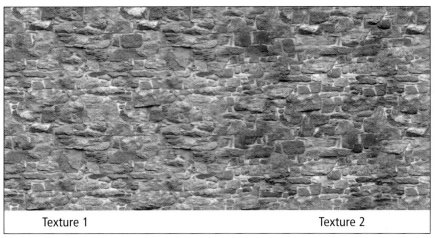

Texture 1   Texture 2

Figure 6.16
The completed textures seamlessly tiled next to one another. Their internal composi-
tions differ, but their borders are the same, thus breaking up texture pattern repetition.

As you can see in Figure 6.16, I've placed the first medieval stone wall texture next to the new texture. The internal composition of both textures is different, but their borders are the same, allowing them to tile seamlessly together and break up pattern repetition. If you continue making a couple more textures this way, you'll have a four-texture, seamlessly tiling set that you can use in a game engine like *Half-Life*, whose engine can randomly tile this set on a large wall.

To use a set of four textures in *Half-Life*, the only thing that you need to do is change the naming convention and size. The maximum texture dimensions in *Half-Life* are 256 × 256 pixels. For instance, the game engine would recognize and utilize a contiguous texture set named like this:

-0medstonewall.bmp

-1medstonewall.bmp

-2medstonewall.bmp

-3medstonewall.bmp

All you need to do is place -# before each file name, where # is a number beginning with 0 and continuing sequentially. See the game engine documentation for details on importing and applying texture sets.

tip

It's a good idea to make a number of similar, tileable stone wall textures with varying saturation and whatnot. This way, you create a library of castle textures that you can use on other walls, such as in the dungeon.

tip

Remember to retain the large version of your textures and save them in Photoshop's PSD format, before you reduce for the game engine. This way, as technology gets better and game engines accept higher resolution images, you can revert to the larger, original version.

Medieval Castle Stone Wall II

The next example demonstrates how to create another, cool medieval stone wall using a single photograph. Then I'm going to add a picture of a stone gargoyle and paste it into a tile, blending it in nicely. Doing so creates two textures: one that can tile seamlessly in a single row along a wall, and one in which the gargoyle can interrupt the pattern. Note that I'm not going to issue a tutorial here; rather, I'm going to display the general steps I've taken to create each step of the texture. If you want to try to follow along, see Figures 6.17 through 6.27 as references. Start by opening the stonewallpic4.jpg image located on the CD-ROM.

Figure 6.17
The stonewallpic4.jpg image, which will serve as the basis for creating the entire texture.

Figure 6.18
Here I've desaturated the image and then darkened it with Image, Adjustments, Brightness/Contrast. Then I made a 256 × 256-pixel selection on the left side.

Figure 6.19
After copying the selection, I created a tileable pattern out of it and filled a 512 × 512-pixel image with it. Here, I've copied a single rectangular selection across the image and applied a drop shadow style.

Figure 6.20
The upper portion of the texture will contain cement enrailments that have a convex shape (upward inner bevel) to them. First I make a single rectangular selection across the top of the image.

Figure 6.21
I make a copy of the selection to a new layer and apply an inner bevel style to that layer. Note that the highlight color for that style is a dark gray.

Figure 6.22
Here I repeat the copy-bevel process, creating a few more enrailments. To some, I also add a drop shadow style to give it more depth.

Figure 6.23
To augment the 3D shapes in the image, I use the Dodge and Burn tools to highlight the tops and shadow the bottoms of the enrailments, respectively. This image represents the completed tiling wall.

Figure 6.24
For a transition texture, I'd like to simply put a blended gargoyle on the enrailment. This image is a picture of a real gargoyle found on a city building in London.

Figure 6.25
I selected the gargoyle out of the original image and pasted it into the image. Then I desaturated it, scaled it, and moved it into place. A few Levels adjustments were necessary as well.

Figure 6.26
Here I used the Burn tool to cancel much of the apparent highlights on the gargoyle. Then I applied a drop shadow style and added some dripping filth behind the head. I made the head symmetrical by copying one-half of the head, mirroring it, and pasting it to the other side.

Figure 6.27
The completed texture set. The gargoyle texture makes a nice transition between the two textures.

This texture could easily port itself over to the modern haunted house genre as well. You'll be building a single door in its entirety; then, at the end, you'll make a copy of it and flip it over as the other door. Instead of creating the wood for the door from scratch, as we did in the previous example, you'll create it from a digital photograph of a table.

Castle Door

This texture is fairly easy but takes a while. Much of it is just pure repetition. For it, I picture those huge English oak doors bound by wrought iron that were so commonplace in the thirteenth century, particularly during the Crusades. Nearly everything was adorned by a cross or crucifix of some sort. The doors I'd like to see also have huge drop handles (knockers) that weigh a gazillion pounds. Figure 6.28 shows the completed texture you'll create.

Figure 6.28
The completed, monstrous doors applied to the castle entrance.

Figure 6.29
Open the `wood_table.jpg` file.

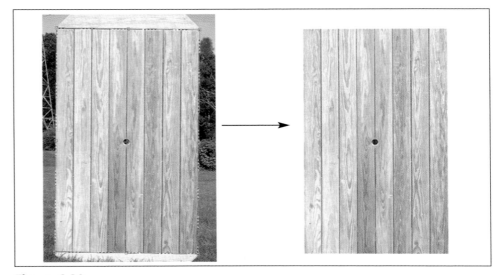

Figure 6.30
Create a selection around the vertical boards of the table, copy the selection, and paste it to a new image.

1. To begin, open the `wood_table.jpg` file located on the CD-ROM; it's shown in Figure 6.29.

2. Grab all the vertical boards that make up the face of the table; this will represent the entire door. To begin, create a selection around the boards using the Rectangular Marquee tool, and then rotate the selection slightly so that the rectangular outline matches the outer edges of the vertical boards using Select, Transform Selection.

3. Copy the selection, close the image, and paste the copied selection to a new Photoshop image. (See Figure 6.30.) The new image inherits the copied image's dimensions.

4. Get rid of the hole in the center of the table by using the Clone Stamp tool with a medium Opacity setting, like 70 percent. (I Alt+clicked a point about one-half inch above the hole, and then sprayed with a small brush over the hole until it was gone.)

5. Adjust the levels a bit to sharpen/darken the image.

6. Choose Image, Adjust, Hue/ Saturation to desaturate the wood's tones. (See Figure 6.31.)

Figure 6.31
Use the Clone Stamp tool to get rid of the hole in the table. Adjust the levels and hue/saturation to suit.

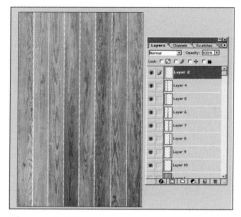

Figure 6.32
Select each board with the Rectangular Marquee tool and create a copy onto its own layer. Make space between each for beveling.

Figure 6.33
Merge the board layers onto a single layer and apply an inner bevel style to them.

Style: Bevel and Emboss
Style: Inner Bevel
Technique: Chisel Soft
Depth: 600%
Direction: Up
Size: 4
Soften: 0
Shading Angle: 72 degrees
Highlight Color: hex# 6B580B
Contour: Cove— Deep contour
Range: 20%

7. Each of the boards needs to be isolated onto its own layer so that you can apply a bevel style to it. Using the Rectangular Marquee tool, create a selection around one board, right-click the selection, and choose Layer Via Copy.

8. Repeat step 7 for the remaining seven boards.

9. Space the boards apart so that a small gap exists between each one. (See Figure 6.32.) This way, the bevels will have room to present themselves.

10. You should have eight layers in the Layers palette that contain individual boards. Go ahead and merge them, *excluding the background layer.*

11. With the layer that contains the boards active, apply an inner bevel style to raise the wood, as shown in Figure 6.33. (I added a Contour style as well.)

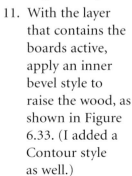

12. Flatten all the layers in the image. You now have the base texture for your door.

13. From here, let's create the rusty, riveted bindings that hold the boards together. I recommend using a picture of something rusty to create the best effect; for this reason, I've provided the file `rusty_metal.jpg` on the CD-ROM. (See Figure 6.34.) You can take samples from this image to create the metal bindings. I took this picture somewhere on the E train subway platform in New York City.

Figure 6.34
Open the `rusty_metal.jpg` image on the CD-ROM, which you'll use to create the metal bindings.

14. Using the Rectangular Marquee tool, make a horizontal, thin selection—roughly the shape

of a binding—on any part of the rusty area in the `rusty_metal.jpg` image.

15. Copy the selection from the `rusty_metal.jpg` image and paste it on the door.

16. Adjust the levels to sharpen/ darken the image a bit. (See Figure 6.35.)

Figure 6.35
Create a selection of rust in the shape of a metal binding, copy it, and paste it to the door.

17. You can make the metal binding appear slightly raised by applying an outer bevel to it. It doesn't take much; just a subtle bevel will do.

18. Using the metal as a base material, use the Elliptical Marquee tool to make a circular rivet. (See Figure 6.36.)

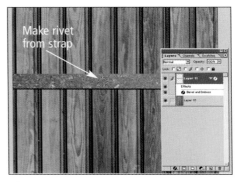

Make rivet from strap

Figure 6.36
Bevel the metal binding to make it a bit 3D. Begin creating a rivet by making a small circular selection on top of the binding.

tip

See the section "Rivets and Screws" in Chapter 2, "Nasty Decals," for detailed information on creating rivets.

19. Right-click the rivet selection and choose Layer Via Copy.

20. Apply an inner bevel style to the new layer (the one with the rivet).

note

You'll need to play around with the inner bevel style's settings a bit to make it appear raised. Just make sure the lighting angle is consistent—that is, the light sources for all styles must come from above.

21. Add a blank layer and merge it with the rivet's layer to get rid of the inner bevel style in the Layers palette, but retain the style in the image. This way, you can duplicate the rivet over and over without caking up the styles.

22. Make copies of the rivet and position them as I have in Figure 6.37.

23. Repeat steps 14–22 to continue forming metal bindings with rivets all around the door as I have done in Figure 6.38. Notice the left side of the door; I applied the same rivet style to a thin rectangular selection, simulating hinges of a sort.

24. Merge all the metal bindings to one layer, but keep them separate from the door itself so that you can make drop shadows and other adjustments later.

25. Let's add a drop handle to the top center of the door. You can do this in several ways. Some people like to use the Path tool to create designs and then fill them with textures; I, on the other hand, use the Alpha channels extensively (outlined here). To begin, create a circular selection using the Elliptical Marquee tool as I have done in Figure 6.39. This will be the base shape of the pattern you'll create.

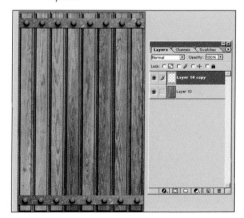

Figure 6.37
Copy the circular rust selection to its own layer and apply an inner-bevel style to raise it. Position multiple copies of the newly created rivet as shown.

Figure 6.38
Repeat the last few steps to continue adding bindings around the door.

Figure 6.39
Start a drop handle by creating a circular selection with the Elliptical Marquee tool.

26. In the Channels palette, start a new channel.

27. The selection should still be active in this new channel; fill it with white.

28. Make a cross pattern by using the Rectangular Marquee tool to cut horizontal and vertical slots out of the shape.

29. Choose Filter, Blur, Gaussian Blur, about 7 pixels.

30. To sharpen the image, choose Image, Adjust, Levels and drag the Shadows and Highlights markers together until the edges of the shape are nice and crisp, as shown in Figure 6.40. (This technique is a great way to create smooth, curved objects.)

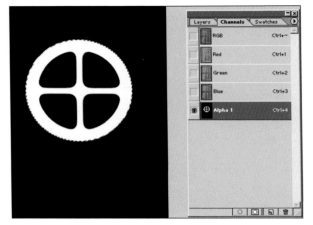

Figure 6.41
Create another circular selection around the existing object and invert it. Ctrl+click the channel to load the selection.

31. Make another circular selection around the existing pattern.

32. Choose Image, Adjust, Invert; you should end up with a white pattern that looks like the one in Figure 6.41. Remember: The white areas in the channel represent the selection boundaries.

33. When the shape in the Alpha channel looks good, Ctrl+click the channel to load the selection.

34. With the selection active, go back to the Layers palette and start a new layer.

35. Fill the selection with a sample of rust from the rusty_metal.jpg image.

36. As you did in steps 17–22, finish the pattern with an outer bevel and some smaller rivets. (See Figure 6.42.)

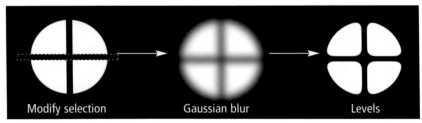

Figure 6.40
Start a new channel and fill the selection with white. Carve the selection to your liking, and then Gaussian Blur it. Use the Levels command to sharpen it back up.

Figure 6.42
On a new layer, fill the selection with rust from the `rusty_metal.jpg` image. Apply an outer bevel and some smaller rivets.

Figure 6.44
Create a circular selection in the shape of a hoop, where the handle will be.

Figure 6.43
Create two small raised surfaces that will support the drop handle.

37. Merge the pattern you just created with the metal binding's layer.

38. In the same way that you created the rivets, create two small raised objects that will support the actual drop handle; Figure 6.43 shows mine.

39. Now for the handle: You're essentially going to make a 3D hoop from scratch (a technique you learned in the "Pipes" and "Rivets and Screws" sections in Chapter 2). Create a circular selection in the shape of a hoop that barely touches both of the raised objects you created in the previous step. (See Figure 6.44.)

40. In the Channels palette, create another new channel.

41. The hoop's selection should still be active; choose Edit, Stroke, about 8 pixels wide.

42. Stroke this selection with white.

43. Ctrl+click the channel to reload the selection.

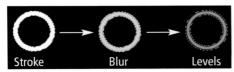

Figure 6.45
Stroke the selection in a new channel. Use the blur-levels technique to create a 3D appearance, and then make a copy of the selection.

44. Choose Filter, Blur, Gaussian Blur, about 5 pixels.

45. With the selection still loaded, adjust the levels (slide the Midtones and Highlights markers together) until you start seeing a 3D shaded hoop. (See Figure 6.45.)

46. Press Ctrl+C to copy the selection.

47. In the Layers palette, start a new layer.

48. With the new layer active, press Ctrl+V to paste the contents from the channel.

49. Adjust the levels again to darken the hoop.

50. Choose Filter, Noise, Add Noise, about 10 percent. (See Figure 6.46.) Now it looks like a weathered, wrought-iron drop handle.

Figure 6.46
Paste the hoop onto a new layer, adjust the levels, and add some noise. Finish it off with a drop shadow.

51. Add a finishing touch by applying a drop shadow to the drop handle.

52. Link and merge the handle's layer and the metal binding's layer. You should now have only two layers: the bindings and drop handle on one layer, with the wooden door on the background layer.

53. Choose Image, Adjust, Curves to correct the colorization and specularity of the metal binding's layer. In Figure 6.47, you can see how I adjusted the graph in the Curves command to tone down the metal and

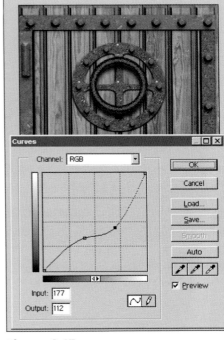

Figure 6.47
Merge the metal layers and adjust the specularity of the layer using the Curves command.

make it look more real. The Curves function is handy for adjusting specular highlights in images.

54. Touch up the entire image using the Burn tool with a low setting, such as 5 percent

Figure 6.48
The completed door texture.

exposure, and a splatter-like brush. This gives the door a nice weathered look. (See Figure 6.48.)

tip

If you burn shadows into the top areas of the wood, the bindings will appear to be floating away from the door. Correct this by undoing it or using the Dodge tool.

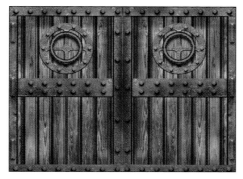

Figure 6.49
Touch up the image using the Burn tool with a low setting. Make a copy of the door, flip it, and align it next to the original.

Figure 6.50
The ominous iron-laden doors displayed in a game.

55. Flatten the image, and increase the Photoshop *canvas* width (not image width) by 100 percent.

56. Make a copy of the door, paste it into the same image, and click Edit, Transform, Flip Horizontal.

57. Position the copy next to the original. (See Figure 6.49.) This completes a double-door texture.

In Figure 6.50, I've placed this texture in a game similar to *Return to Castle Wolfenstein*. It blends in quite well, methinks.

Draconis

In these last sections, I'm flipping over to fantasy. In the next few tutorials, I'll show you how to make some critical texture objects for a 3D dragon model, namely eyes, teeth, and scales. See Figure 6.64 at the end of these three sections to view a completed dragon model using these textures.

Dragon's Eye

I'm borrowing from a couple of tutorials in this book to complete a dragon's eye. For this exercise, you'll need a completed Blast Mark decal from Chapter 2, as well as the second Lava texture example from Chapter 7, "Planetary Textures." Either complete those yourself or open the `blastmark.jpg` and `lava2.jpg` files located on the CD-ROM.

1. The second lava example from Chapter 7 will make for a great, eerie dragon's eyeball base texture. (See Figure 6.51.)

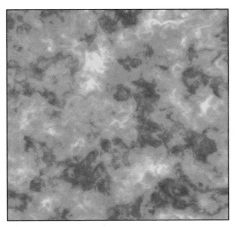

Figure 6.51
Create a base lava texture from Chapter 7 or open the `lava2.jpg` image on the CD-ROM.

2. Use the Elliptical Marquee tool to create and copy an eyeball-shaped selection from the lava image. Then create a new image and paste this selection into it. (See Figure 6.52.)

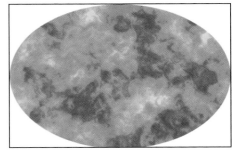

Figure 6.52
Select an eyeball shape out of the lava texture and paste it into a new image.

Figure 6.53
Apply the Spherize filter a few times to make the eyeball more rounded.

3. To the eyeball, apply Filter, Distort, Spherize, 100 percent. Apply this filter several times. (See Figure 6.53.)

4. Now for the pupil. Open the `blastmark.jpg` file (or create one of your own). The image is white on black; we need the white's selection. Go to the Channels palette, and Ctrl+click on the RGB channel to load the selection. Press Ctrl+C to copy it. Then go back to the eyeball image and, in the Channels palette, create a new channel and Ctrl+V to paste the blast mark.

5. The selection should still be active. Click on the background layer in the layer's palette. Move the selection to the center of the eyeball. Press D to reset the Color Control Panel, and then press Alt+Backspace to fill the selection with black. Press Alt+Backspace a couple more times to darken the pupil. (See Figure 6.54.)

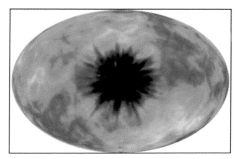

Figure 6.54
Use the `blastmark.jpg` decal made from Chapter 2 to create a black pupil.

6. Now to gloss up the eyeball. Press Ctrl+D to deselect the active selection. Ctrl+click the eyeball layer to load the eyeball's shape, and start a new layer. On this layer, with the selection still active, create a Radial Gradient that begins from the upper-right area of the eye and ends at the lower-left area. (See Figure 6.55.) This will be our blending mode mask, used much in the same way that game engines use black-to-white decals to make glass.

7. Change the Blending Mode of this new layer to Hard Light. Adjust the curves of the layer as I have done in Figure 6.56 to complete the eyeball.

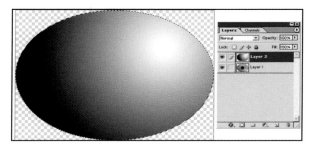

Figure 6.55
Create a Radial Gradient on a new layer in the shape of the eyeball.

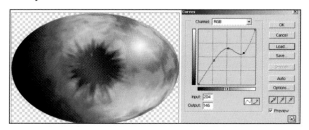

Figure 6.56
Change the blending mode to Hard Light, and adjust the curves to complete the eyeball.

Dragon's Tooth

This is a quick way to get a nice, rough dragon's tooth.

1. Start a new 512 × 512-pixel image, with a resolution of 512.

2. Set the background layer to transparent.

3. Use the Lasso tool to create a tall, slender, tooth shape on the background layer.

4. Fill the tooth with a light beige mix of the Clouds filter, as shown in Figure 6.57. (I used hex# BEB4A0 and hex# ABA18D for the foreground and background colors for this filter.)

5. Keeping the selection active, use the Burn tool to burn some darkness into the base and edges of the tooth.

6. Lightly spray a bit of red on the base, simulating the gum line or perhaps blood stains.

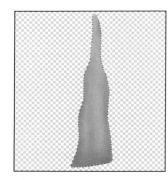

Figure 6.57
Create a tooth-shaped selection and use the Clouds filter to fill it with beige. Burn the edges and add some red to the base.

7. Make a copy of this layer. You should now have two tooth layers in the Layers palette.

8. Ctrl+click the tooth layer to load its selection. Press Ctrl+C to copy it.

9. In the Channels palette, create a new channel.

10. In the new channel, press Ctrl+V to paste the tooth.

11. With the new channel still active, choose Filter, Noise, Add Noise, about 10 percent; then apply Filter, Noise, Median, 1 pixel. (See Figure 6.58.) You'll use this channel as a bump map for the second tooth layer.

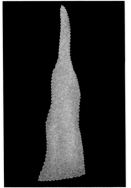

Figure 6.58
Create a copy of the tooth layer, and place a copy of the tooth layer in a new channel for a bump map. Add noise to the channel as well.

13. Go back to the Layers palette and click on the top tooth layer. Choose Filter, Render, Lighting Effects, and use the Alpha 1 channel as a displacement map.

14. Change this layer's blending mode from Normal to Overlay. Flatten the image to merge the layers. Finally, apply an inner bevel to the tooth to give it a nice, 3D curve. (See Figure 6.59.)

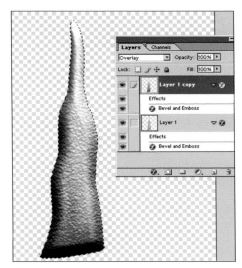

Figure 6.59
Render the top tooth layer with the Lighting Effects filter, using the alpha channel as a displacement map. Change this layer to Overlay, flatten the image, and apply an inner bevel to finish the effect.

Dragon's Skin

I came up with this texture by accident; I was trying to create a good rock texture, but out popped a perfect texture for a dragon's skin (or Basilisk or Maiasaur).

1. Start a new 512 × 512-pixel RGB image.

2. Set your foreground color to a slimy-green, such as hex#D5E043, and your background to a reddish-brown, such as hex#783522.

3. Choose Filter, Render, Clouds. (See Figure 6.60.)

Filter: Render, Clouds
Foreground: hex#D5E043
Background: hex#783522

Figure 6.60
Apply the Clouds filter using green and reddish-brown colors.

4. In the Channels palette, create a new alpha channel.

5. Apply the Filter, Render, Clouds filter to the new alpha channel.

6. Choose Filter, Render, Difference Clouds; press Ctrl+F to apply the filter several times until you get a nice blend of black and white. (See Figure 6.61.)

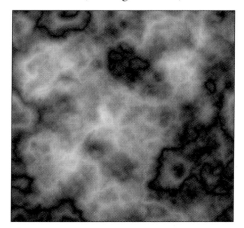

Figure 6.61
Create a new channel and apply both the Clouds and Difference Clouds filters.

7. Choose Filter, Noise, Add Noise, about 5 percent. (Be sure Gaussian and Monochromatic are checked off within the filter.)

8. Click the background layer in the Layers palette.

Filter: Render, Lighting Effects
Light Type: Directional (from above)
Intensity: 24
Focus: 63
Gloss: 75
Material: 96
Exposure: 0
Ambience: 8
Texture Channel: Alpha 1
Height: 100

Figure 6.62
Render the background layer using the Alpha 1 channel as a displacement map.

Figure 6.63
Apply the Craquelure filter for an added touch.

9. Choose Filter, Render, Lighting Effects, using the Alpha 1 channel as a displacement map. (See Figure 6.62.)

You can polish off this texture by using Filter, Texture, Craquelure if you're looking for a more scaly or cracked-skin appearance. (See Figure 6.63.)

Figure 6.64 shows the three dragon textures applied to a 3D dragon model.

Figure 6.64
The dragon textures applied to a 3D model.

Fiery Text Using the Black Body Palette

Black Body is an indexed color mode that displays a palette of colors based on the different colors that a blackbody radiator emits as it is heated—from black to red, orange, yellow, and white. At least, that's Adobe's description of it. Basically, the Black Body mode converts the grayscale colors in an indexed image into a fiery spectrum of colors, depending on the shade of gray in the image. This next tutorial demonstrates a quick way to create glowing text (or any other grayscale object, for that matter) that would look cool on a game cover or other piece of artwork. Consider using this tutorial to create fire in general.

1. Create a new 512 × 512 RGB color image with a transparent background. Fill it with pure black.

2. Create some pure white text. Scale and center the text to your liking, and then choose Layer, Rasterize, Type. This rasterizes

the type and makes it editable. (See Figure 6.65.)

3. Make two copies of this text layer, making a total of three text layers.

4. To the bottom text layer, apply Filter, Blur, Radial Blur. Then, to the middle text layer, apply Filter, Blur, Motion Blur, vertically. (See Figure 6.66.)

5. Click Image, Mode, Grayscale. Click Merge Layers when it prompts you to.

6. Click Image, Mode, Indexed Color. Click OK when it prompts you to flatten the image.

7. Click Image, Mode, Color Table and, from the Table list, select Black Body. Your grayscale colors in the image are replaced with the black body palette. (See Figure 6.67.)

Figure 6.67
Change the image mode to Grayscale and then Indexed Color. Then change the Color Table to Black Body to attain the fiery text.

Figure 6.65
Create some white text on a black background. Rasterize the text.

Filter: Blur, Radial Blur
Amount: 60
Blur Method: Zoom
Quality: Good
Filter: Blur, Motion Blur
Angle: 90
Distance: 20 pixels

Figure 6.66
Apply a Radial Blur to the bottom text layer and then a vertical Motion Blur to the middle text layer.

You can make some minor adjustments to make the image look more fire-like, such as Image, Adjust, Levels, Curves, or Hue/Saturation. In Figure 6.68, I did this and added a Lens Flare filter for an added effect.

Figure 6.68
Adjust the image using Levels, Curves, or Hue/Saturation commands.

Wizard's Orb

This final tutorial really fits into the fantasy category. The Polar Coordinates filter technique is a common way to create textures that require a global image. This filter is used particularly in games for making skyboxes (the sky textures you see when walking around outdoors in a 3D game). This example utilizes the same Polar Coordinates technique, only creating a glass orb from scratch with no base texture. I'd like to thank Vahn for inspiring this one.

Figure 6.69
Apply a diagonal lens flare.

1. Create a new 512 × 512 RGB color image with a transparent background. Fill it with pure black.

2. Click Filter, Render, Lens Flare. Apply a lens flare as I have done in Figure 6.69.

3. Click Filter, Distort, Polar Coordinates, and perform a Polar to Rectangular distortion. (See Figure 6.70.)

4. Click Edit, Transform, Flip Vertical.

Filter: Render, Lens Flare
Brightness: 115%
Flare Center: Upper-left, diagonal
Lens Type: 105mm Prime

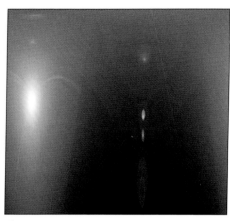

Figure 6.70
Apply a Polar to Rectangular distort filter.

5. Click Filter, Distort, Polar Coordinates, and perform the reverse—Rectangular to Polar distortion. (See Figure 6.71.) The orb comes into focus.

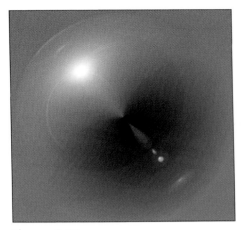

Figure 6.71
Flip the image vertically, and then apply a
Rectangular to Polar distort filter.

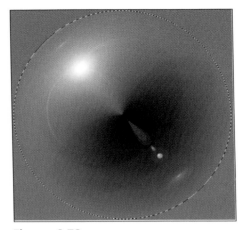

Figure 6.72
Select the orb in the image by using the
Elliptical Marquee tool.

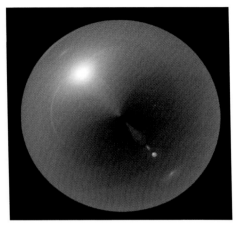

Figure 6.73
You can copy/paste the orb onto a new
layer, make adjustments, and change its
color by using the Variations command.

6. Now you just need to extract
   the orb. Use the Elliptical Marquee tool to select the orb out
   of the image. Hold down Shift
   when doing this to create a perfect circle. (See Figure 6.72.)

7. After the selection is in place,
   invert the selection (Select,
   Inverse) and copy it to a new
   layer. You can now adjust the
   Curves to enhance the shininess
   and change the color by choosing Image, Adjust, Variations.
   (See Figure 6.73.)

Summary

There are many different ways to create rustic stone wall and floor textures. In this chapter, I demonstrated
how to manipulate digital photographs of stone walls to create base
stone wall textures. These textures,
when produced properly, can be tiled
seamlessly across large surfaces to
produce a realistic environment.
However, sometimes it helps to break
up repetition if you create a *transition
set*, or similar textures whose edges
blend together seamlessly.

Photographs are also great for assist-
ing in texture details, such as the door
texture I demonstrated. That texture
came to life with pictures of rust and
wood. This is the most common way
to create textures for video games.
The textures presented in this chapter
fit perfectly in a medieval world.
However, I primarily used *Return to
Castle Wolfenstein* to present the textures in a practical gaming environment.

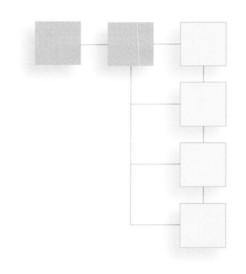

CHAPTER 7

PLANETARY TEXTURES

Ad astra per aspera...

To the stars, through difficulties...

This section is dedicated to a handful of textures that pertain primarily to any geometry belonging to a planet, be it Earth or another large oblate spheroid. Some of these textures are meant to be tiled uniquely upon a single mesh or plane, whereas others can (and should) be grouped in a texture set of similarity because the same image tiled dozens of times can be quite monotonous. I'll show you how to create the following textures:

- Scorched earth
- Two types of hot lava, one of which can be considered boiling acid
- Cooled lava
- Mars rock
- Mars or lunar surface
- Polaris, the creation of a star

Scorched Earth

This is a quick but effective ground tile that's useful for stretching itself over medium-sized distances of around 50 meters square. The nature of Photoshop's Clouds filter in this case automatically makes this a seamless texture, and you might be able to get away with tiling this just several times in each direction. You can play around with the colors of the different blended layers to achieve other terrains such as grass and dirt as well.

Follow these steps to create the scorched earth texture:

1. Start a new 1024 × 1024 pixel, 1024 dpi, RGB color image.

2. Fill the background layer with the Clouds filter using hex# 302C2B and hex# 4E3E31 as the foreground and background colors in the Color Control Panel.

3. Apply the Difference Clouds filter a few times until you get a nice mix of these dark terrain colors. (See Figure 7.1.)

4. Create a new layer and fill this one with the Clouds filter using hex# 795F3C and hex# 383530. Apply the Difference Clouds filter to this a few times as well.

5. Double-click the top layer to open the Layer Style panel. The default style option is the Blending Options panel, which allows you to blend layers and create knockout effects. In the bottom Blend If section, slide the left marker in the This Layer slider to about 60, allowing the background layer to slowly bleed through. (See Figure 7.2.)

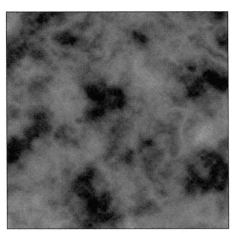

Filter: Render, Clouds/Difference Clouds
Foreground: hex# 302C2B
Background: hex# 4E3E31

Figure 7.1
Use the Clouds and Difference Clouds filters to mix some dark earth colors together.

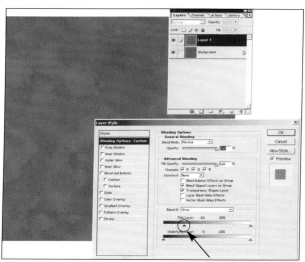

Figure 7.2
Use the Blending options in the Layer Style panel to blend the two cloudy layers.

Filter: Render, Clouds/Difference Clouds
Foreground: hex# 795F3C
Background: hex# 383530

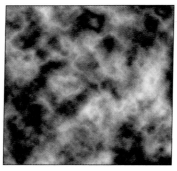

Figure 7.3
Use the Clouds and Difference Clouds filters to create a height map in a new channel.

you created as a height map, thereby creating terrain bumps throughout the image.

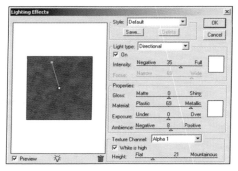

Figure 7.4
Apply the Lighting Effects filter using Alpha 1 as the texture channel.

6. With the top layer selected, merge the two layers (Ctrl+E).

7. Start a new channel in the Channels palette and apply the Clouds filter.

8. Now apply the Difference Clouds filter a few times. This channel will be your alpha channel for a height map. (See Figure 7.3.)

9. Go back to the Layers palette and select the background layer. Chose Filter, Render, Lighting

Effects, using the settings as I have in Figure 7.4. Make sure to use a Directional Light (left side of image) as the lighting source; otherwise, your image will flood with light on the top portion, making it untileable. Direct the lighting source so that it points top-down and at a slight angle, as I have done. Also make sure you use the newly created clouds channel (Alpha 1) as the Texture Channel. This filter uses this channel

10. Your texture is almost complete. I want to dirty it up some more, so try adding another channel in the Channels palette and applying the Clouds filter to it. Apply the Difference Clouds filter a few times, just as you did to the first channel you created. Now click Image, Adjustments, Levels, and slide the left marker (Shadows) over to the right until much of the channel is flooded with black. (See Figure 7.5.)

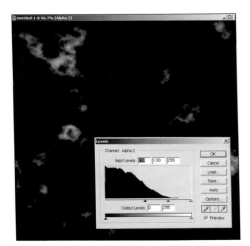

Figure 7.5
Create another channel and fill it with
Clouds and Difference Clouds. Adjust the
levels to flood the channel a bit with black.

11. Ctrl+click this channel to select
    its opacity (white areas).

12. Go back to the Layers palette
    and click on the background
    layer. Press D to reset the Color
    Control Panel, and then press
    Alt+Backspace once or twice to
    fill the selection. This adds
    some random scarring to the
    texture. (See Figure 7.6.)
    Finally, adjust your levels a bit
    to your satisfaction. This can be
    your final texture, and it's ran-
    domly tileable.

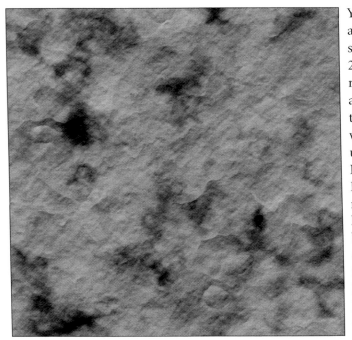

Figure 7.6
Load the new channel's opacity and use this selection to dirty up
your texture.

tip

More often than not, you'll have to
adjust the levels or saturation of your
final image to achieve the best texturing effect. My textures would stick out
like a neon sign if I didn't darken them
or desaturate the colors (Image, Adjustments, Hue/Saturation).

You can now palettize
and reduce this tile to
something like 256 ×
256 (using Bilinear
resampling) for use in
a game. The important
thing to remember
with this texture is the
use of the Lighting
Effects filter. Using the
Directional Light
mimics an ambient
lighting source, there-
by evenly lighting the
entire image, unlike
the Spot or Omni
lights, which create a
lighting imbalance
from one side to the
other. In the latter case,
the texture's edges
would still match up
during tiling, but you
would see an obvious light/dark seam
between tiles. Figure 7.7 shows this tile
sprayed on a mountain side in the
Torque game engine.

Figure 7.7
The completed scorched earth texture in the Torque game engine.

GarageGames ©2000-2004

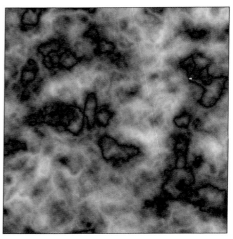

Figure 7.8
Apply the Clouds filter, and then apply the Difference Clouds filter several times to a new alpha channel.

Hot Lava

I invented this texture by accident. Here's how it's done:

1. Fill a new 1024 × 1024 pixel, 1024 dpi RGB color image with pure black.

tip

You are recording your texture implementations in the Actions palette, aren't you?

2. In the Channels palette, create a new channel.

3. Press D to reset the foreground and background colors to white and black, respectively.

4. Click Filter, Render, Clouds.

5. Click Filter, Render, Difference Clouds. Press Ctrl+F several times to reapply this filter until you get a nice mix of black and white. (See Figure 7.8.)

6. Click Image, Adjustments, Levels.

7. Slide the Shadows marker to the right a bit to flood out the black areas. (You want a nice, thick filling of black, which you'll fill with molten-hot colors. (See Figure 7.9.)

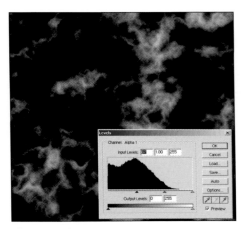

Figure 7.9
Adjust the levels in the alpha channel to enhance the shadows.

8. In the Layers palette, click on the background layer to select it.

9. Click Filter, Render, Lighting Effects, making sure Alpha 1 is the selected texture channel. Scale the Directional Light source down a bit in the filter's preview area. (This makes the light source shine more overhead, eliminating unnecessary shadows.) See Figure 7.10.

10. Now it's time to make a proper fill selection for the molten lava. I frequently use alpha

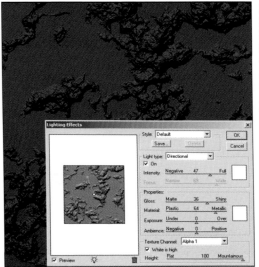

Figure 7.10
Apply the Lighting Effects filter to the background layer, using the alpha channel as a displacement map.

channels to store selections, so we'll do that here. Using the Channels palette, make a copy of the Alpha 1 channel. (Click and drag it to the Create New Channel icon.)

11. Invert this new copy by clicking Image, Adjustments, Invert (Ctrl+I).

Filter: Render, Lighting Effects
Light Type: Directional
Intensity: 47
Focus: 69
Gloss: −36
Material: −64
Exposure: 0
Ambience: 0
Texture Channel: Alpha 1
Height: 100

12. Click Image, Adjustments, Levels, and slide the Shadows marker (at the far left) all the way to the far right. This creates 100 percent contrast between black and white. (See Figure 7.11.)

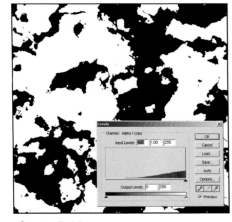

Figure 7.11
Make a copy of the Alpha 1 channel, invert it, and adjust the levels to bring out all the white.

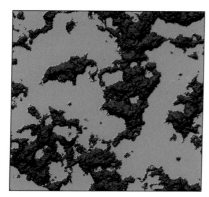

Figure 7.12
Select the opacity of the new alpha channel and fill this selection with a reddish-orange color on a new layer.

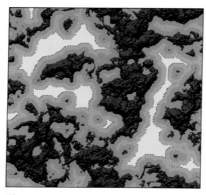

Figure 7.13
Reduce the selection area, fill with orange, reduce again, and then fill with yellow.

Figure 7.14
Blur the molten lava layer with the Gaussian Blur filter.

13. Ctrl+click the new alpha channel to select all of its white.

14. Go back to the Layers palette and start a new layer.

15. The selection should now be on the new layer; fill the selection with a reddish-orange color, such as hex# FB2900. (See Figure 7.12.)

16. Now let's make the center of the molten lava appear very hot. With the selection still active (you can always go back to the new alpha channel and Ctrl+click it to restore the selection area), click Select,

Modify, Contract, and enter a value of 20 pixels.

17. Fill this new area with an orange color, such as hex# FB5900.

18. Again, click Select, Modify, Contract, and enter a value of 20 pixels.

19. Fill this selection with a bright yellow, such as hex# FBF200. (See Figure 7.13.)

20. To this top layer, apply Filter, Blur, Gaussian Blur, with a radius of about 15 pixels.

21. Double-click this layer to bring up the Styles screen, and add a red-colored Outer Glow style. (See Figure 7.14.)

Filter: Blur, Gaussian Blur
Radius: 15 pixels

This is an effective technique for reproducing lava, both hot and cold. You might think that offsetting this for a tile will be a bit cumbersome because it has so much detail, but this isn't the case. When you applied the Difference Clouds filter to the first alpha channel, the filter applied itself as a tileable offset; the rest of the texture was based on that original channel. It's up to you to fix the colors in an offset—try merging the layers and then choosing Filter, Other, Offset with a Horizontal and Vertical shift of 512 pixels. Then use the Healing Brush tool (instead of the Clone Stamp tool) to fix the seams in the hot lava.

tip

This first lava texture is a perfect candidate for creating a tile set. See Chapter 6, "Medieval/Fantasy Textures," for an example of creating seamlessly tiling sets that consist of similar textures, all of which can be rotated in any direction, to help break up repetitive patterns.

Hot Lava 2, or Boiling Acid

This texture is much faster than the previous one but without the floating lava rock effect. The texture packages created by Shane Caudle in the *Unreal Tournament* game engine have some lava images similar to this one, and if you have ever played *Quake II*, you would have seen some boiling acid pits that looked like this as well.

1. Start a new 1024 × 1024 pixel, 1024 dpi RGB color image.

2. Set the foreground color to hex# A42E04 and the background color to hex# E45C05. Apply the Clouds filter to the Background layer. This will be a nice reddish-orange base for the lava.

3. Apply the Difference Clouds filter about four times. You'll see the layer go dark twice, but then you'll get a nice choppy blend of the colors. You can adjust your levels here a bit to darken the image if you want.

4. Now apply Filter, Sharpen, Unsharp Mask. This contrasts the pixel color variations in the image. (See Figure 7.15.)

5. Start a new layer. Apply the Clouds filter using hex# FCDE13 and hex# FCB30C, and then apply the Difference Clouds filter five times. This creates a yellowish-orange mix on top of the Background layer. (See Figure 7.16.)

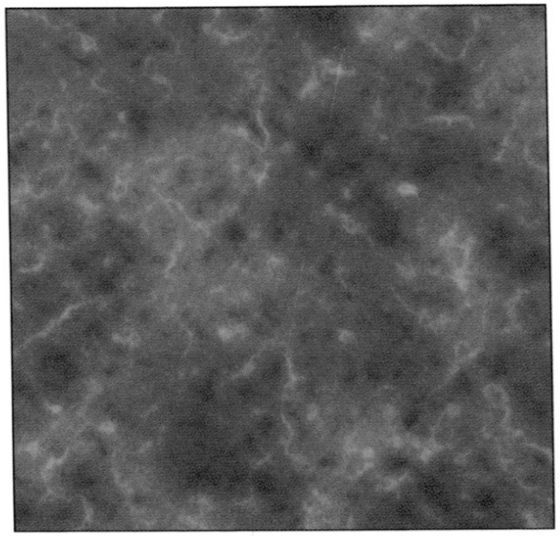

Filter: Render, Clouds/Difference Clouds
Foreground: hex# A42E04
Background: hex# E45C05
Filter: Unsharp Mask
Amount: 400%
Radius: 17 pixels
Threshold: 14 pixels

Figure 7.15
Apply the Clouds and Difference Clouds filters using a reddish-orange mix of colors. Use the Unsharp Mask filter to enhance the pixel color variations.

Figure 7.16
Apply the Clouds and Difference Clouds filters again on a new layer using a yellowish-orange mix of colors.

6. In the Layers palette, reduce this new layer's Opacity to about 20 percent, and set the Blending Mode to Screen.

7. Start a third layer, and set this layer's Blending Mode to Color Dodge. Press D to reset your Color Control Panel, and apply the Clouds filter. Then apply the Difference Clouds filter a few times or until your image has a nice blend of molten lava with bright yellow hot spots. (See Figure 7.17.) Cool, huh? I

Filter: Render, Clouds/Difference Clouds
Foreground: hex# FCDE13
Background: hex# FCB30C

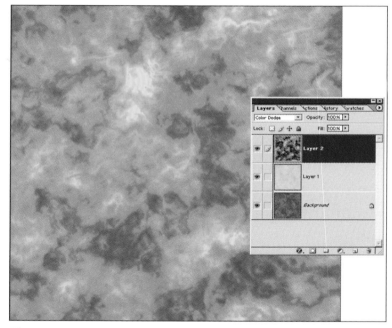

Figure 7.17
Make a third layer, filling it with the Clouds and Difference Clouds filters using black and white. Setting this layer to Color Dodge makes the lava come to life.

think this could also easily pass for boiling acid on a dynamic surface in a game level.

Before you make any final level adjustments or reduce or palettize your texture, be sure to flatten the image to properly merge all the layers. Figure 7.18 shows this texture bubbling away in a game.

Figure 7.18
The completed lava/acid texture in action.

1. Start a new 1024 × 1024-pixel image.

2. Press D to reset the Color Control Panel to black and white.

3. Choose Filter, Render, Clouds.

4. Choose Filter, Stylize, Find Edges. This tells Photoshop to create significant borders where there are definitive transitions in the image.

5. Adjust the levels to bring out your texture. First slide the Midtones marker almost all the way to the right, and then slowly slide the Shadows marker to the right until you get something like what's shown in Figure 7.19.

tip

Sometimes merging one layer with another below it (using Ctrl+E) can result in a loss of blending or other color information. To avoid this, first link the two layers, and then press Ctrl+E to merge them.

Cooled Lava

You could create cold lava by repeating steps 1–9 of the first lava example in this chapter, but you might have to make a slight modification with step 6. Instead of flooding out the black with the Shadows slider in the Levels panel, you could mess with the Midtones and Highlights sliders a bit to enhance the ridges in the final rendering.

The next tutorial, composed of just a few quick steps, produces another type of cooled lava flow that appears somewhat elegant:

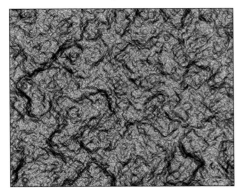

Figure 7.19
Finish the cooled lava texture by adjusting the levels.

Mars Rock

The colors used in this tutorial are great for use on a Martian surface, but use your own for other environments. This texture can be put on canyon walls, mountains, and wrapped around boulders.

1. Start a new 1024 × 1024-pixel RGB image.

2. Select any foreground and background you want; this will be the mineral representation in the rock. For Mars rock, I use rusty colors that involve some sort of reddish-brown, such as hex# A62801 and hex# C46C04.

3. Choose Filter, Render, Clouds; the results are shown in Figure 7.20.

4. Using the Channels palette, start a new channel.

5. Choose Filter, Render, Difference Clouds, and then press Ctrl+F a few times to repeat this action. Do this until the black-and-white mix is somewhat even. (See Figure 7.21.) This will be your displacement map when you render the mineral layer—that is, the whiter areas will represent the high spots on the texture, and the blacker areas will represent the low spots.

6. In the Layers palette, click on the background layer to make it the current working layer.

7. Click Filter, Render, Lighting Effects using Alpha 1 as the texture channel. Again, use a Directional Light that points top-down, at a slight angle. You should end up with a nice rock texture like mine in Figure 7.22.

Figure 7.20
Apply the Clouds filter with a rusty colored foreground and background.

Filter: Render, Clouds
Foreground: hex# A62801
Background: hex# C46C04

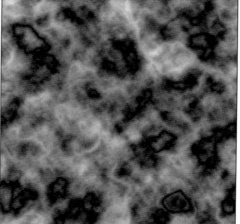

Figure 7.21
Start a new channel and apply the Difference Clouds filter several times.

tip

Try playing around with all the sliders in the Lighting Effects filter to produce an enormous variety of effects, from making the texture rock-like, to bubbly plastic, to lizard skin.

Figure 7.22
Click the Lighting Effects filter and use the Alpha 1 channel as a displacement map.

Filter: Render, Lighting Effects
Light Type: Directional
Intensity: 29
Focus: 69
Gloss: −29
Material: −69
Exposure: 0
Ambience: 0
Texture Channel: Alpha 1
Height: 100

Mars/Lunar Surface Using NASA Planetary Data System Image Maps

Planetary surfaces are hard to do from scratch. Instead, try using real image maps taken from NASA satellites. In this example, I've downloaded some free images from http://pds-imaging. jpl.nasa. gov/, the NASA Planetary Data System. Here, I'll use these as displacement maps to create a seamlessly tileable Mars/lunar texture set,

based on Mars images. I specifically got these at http://pdsmaps. wr.usgs.gov/ PDS/public/explorer/html/marsintm. htm; just click anywhere on the global map of Mars, click on the Double Size by Degrees button, and save the image to disk. For this example, I grabbed four images, each separated by about 10 degrees longitude and latitude, so I could link all four together for one giant 1024 × 1024 map.

1. Start a new 1024 × 1024 pixel, 1024 dpi color image.

2. Either download four 512 pixel images from one of the sites listed earlier (make sure they are neighboring images) or open the files `marsmap01.jpg` through `marsmap04.jpg`. On each of these images, press Ctrl+A to select the entire image, Ctrl+C to copy it, and

then go back to the new 1024 × 1024 image and press Ctrl+V to paste it. Move each layer so that they line up as best as you can. (See Figure 7.23.)

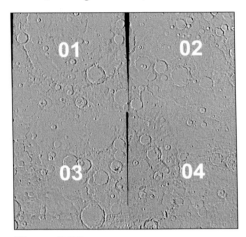

Figure 7.23
Open and tile the four marsmap images from the CD-ROM onto a new image.

3. Click Layer, Flatten Image to merge all the layers to the background layer.

4. Use the Clone Stamp tool to get rid of the black areas *on the inside of the image only*. Work diligently and try not to mess up the existing craters in the image.

5. Use the Crop tool to crop as much of the lunar map as possible without going into the white areas outside of the four map edges. Make your selection by holding down both Ctrl and Shift to create a perfect square selection. (See Figure 7.24.)

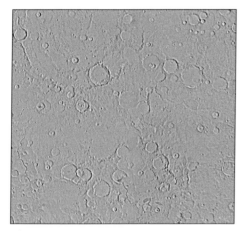

Figure 7.24
Flatten the image, and use the Clone Stamp tool to get rid of the black areas.

6. Click Image, Image Size, and change the image size back to 1024 × 1024 pixels. The image will stretch a little, but not enough to distort anything. You can apply Filter, Sharpen to make it a bit more crisp.

This map is ready to be made tileable by choosing the Offset filter, or you can separate the four 512 × 512-pixel quadrants into separate tile maps to create your own map set. Figure 7.25 shows this entire map wrapped around a 3D sphere; it's not bad for a moon.

Figure 7.25
The four blended maps wrapped around a 3D sphere.

Enhancing the Map: Creating Your Own Custom Shader

Although the lunar map looks okay for a small moon, I still think it's pretty boring. Advanced model texturing almost always involves the use of shaders—that is, a composition of layered textures that each has its own effect on the final rendering. For instance, in a modeling program such as 3D Studio Max, you could create a base material layer that consists only of a blend of colors, add a bump map layer for displacement effects, add a specular layer for shininess, and so on. Let's do something like that in Photoshop to make the terrain more Martian.

1. Start a new 1024 × 1024-pixel image.

2. Fill the background layer with the Clouds and Difference Clouds filters, using a medium tan mix, such as hex# 6D553B and hex# 967B59.

3. Either use your moon map you created previously or open the lunarmap.jpg file located on the CD-ROM. Press Ctrl+A to select everything in this map and then Ctrl+C to copy it. Close this file, and click on the background layer of the new tan image. Press Ctrl+V to paste the moon map on top of the background layer.

4. The moon map is basically grayscale, which will work

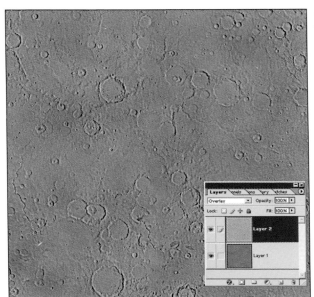

Figure 7.26
Blend the moon map created earlier with a tan background layer using the Overlay blending option.

perfectly with some of the blending options in Photoshop. Set this new layer's blending mode to Overlay. (See Figure 7.26.) Cool, huh? The features on the map are now blended with the background layer.

5. You could stop here and apply this texture to a 3D model, but I'd like to take it a bit further by adding a small amount of

Filters: Clouds / Difference Clouds
Foreground: hex# 6D553B
Background: hex# 967B59

clouds. (Mars does have some clouds in its atmosphere, doesn't it?) Add a new layer on top of everything and set this layer's blending mode to Screen.

6. Press D to reset the Color Control Panel. Apply the Clouds filter and then the Difference Clouds filters several times. Notice that only the white

cloudy areas show through on the map. Now adjust this layer's opacity down to about 50 percent. (See Figure 7.27.)

Now we're getting somewhere! In Figure 7.27, I opted to add another layer behind everything that was merely an inverted black-and-white Clouds layer, and I set the tan layer's blending mode to Multiply. This just created a few dirty patches in the soil

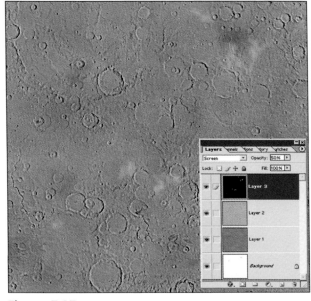

Figure 7.27
Add some clouds to the texture by creating a new layer and applying the Clouds and Difference Clouds filters. Set this layer's blending mode to Screen.

for an added effect. (Open the mars.psd file on the CD-ROM to see my version of the final image.) Basically, this is a hand-made version of a shader that a 3D program or game engine could render. Figure 7.28 shows this texture wrapped around a sphere and rendered in 3D Studio Max.

Figure 7.28
The final Martian texture, rendered on a sphere in 3D Studio Max.

Polaris

This last example is just for fun, and it's totally cool. Here I'll show you how to make clever use of the second lava texture in this chapter to create a flame-engulfed star. I'd like to thank Raptor from Eyeball Design for this one; I merged my ideas with his sun tutorial.

1. If you don't have your lava/acid texture handy, either create one from the example earlier on or open the lava2.jpg file located in the Chapter 7 folder on the CD-ROM.

2. Use the Elliptical Marquee tool to create a perfect circular selection in the center of the lava texture. (See Figure 7.29.) Do this by holding down both Shift and Ctrl while dragging from the center of the image.

3. Press Ctrl+C to copy this selection to the Clipboard.

4. Start a new 512 × 512 pixel, 512 dpi RBG color image.

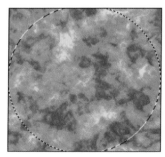

Figure 7.29
Create a circular selection in the middle of the lava/acid texture.

5. Press D to reset the Color Control Panel to black and white.

6. Press Alt+Backspace to fill the background layer with black.

7. Press Ctrl+V to paste the circular lava selection onto a new layer.

8. Ctrl+click the circular lava layer to select its opacity. From now on, I'll call this layer the sun layer.

9. Click Filter, Distort, Spherize. This will bloat the sun to make it appear more spherical. (See Figure 7.30.) You can apply this filter once more if you want, making it even more bloated. Make sure you apply this filter with the sun selected, or all it will do is enhance its diameter!

Filter:
Distort, Spherize
Amount:
100%
Mode:
Normal

Figure 7.30
Ctrl+click the sun layer and apply the Spherize filter.

10. Double-click the sun layer to open the Layer Style screen and add a red-orange Outer Glow using the settings I have listed.

11. Click on the background layer and start a new layer. This puts a layer between the background and the sun.

12. With the sun selection still active on the new blank layer (if it's not active, just Ctrl+click the sun layer), fill this selection with black. To this layer, apply another Outer Glow style using the same style settings as before, but use a yellow-orange color for the glow. (See Figure 7.31.)

You should now have a nice glowing halo around your sun.

13. Now for the kicker. Press Ctrl+D to deselect any active selections. Create a new layer on top of all the layers. Press D to reset the Color Control Panel to black and white. Now set this layer's blending mode to Color Dodge.

14. To this new layer, apply the Clouds filter. Cool, huh? You're not done yet. Now apply the Difference Clouds filter several times or until you're satisfied with the quality of your solar flares.

15. Finally (and this is optional), Ctrl+click the original sun layer to load its opacity, and with the top Clouds layer selected, press Delete. (See Figure 7.32.) This is a simple but cool image that would look great on the cover of a game title. Note that you can also apply another Color Dodged Clouds/Difference Clouds layer on top of everything again to further enhance the flares.

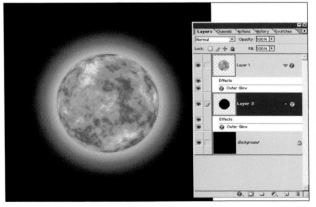

Styles: Outer Glows
Blend Mode: Screen
Opacity: 75%
Noise: 0 %
Colors: hex# FD2704 and hex# FEB70B
Technique: Softer
Spread: 20%
Size: 80 pixels
Range: 60%
Jitter: 0%

Figure 7.31
Apply Outer Glow styles to the sun layers.

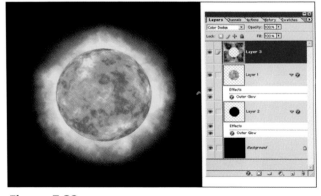

Figure 7.32
Make a new layer on top of everything, set it to Color Dodge, and apply the Clouds and Difference Clouds filters to create solar flares.

Summary

Ground textures are among the easiest to create, using only a handful of filters and minimal artistic skills. Photoshop's Cloud filters are useful in creating random blends of colors that also happen to be seamlessly tileable, making for efficient and realistic ground textures that require little or no cleanup. Cloud filters in this chapter were also employed to create excellent 3D effects in the resultant textures by using them as displacement maps in alpha channels. With only slight variations, the texturing examples presented here can produce an infinite amount of texturing possibilities, from ground cover to rock skin, planetary surfacing, and even animal skin.

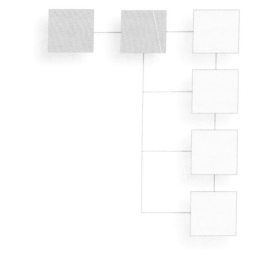

CHAPTER 8

Sci-Fi Textures

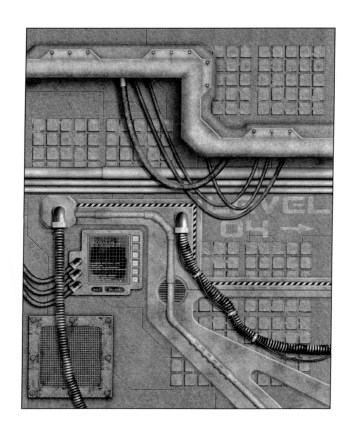

Fidenti animo futura intueor...

I have every confidence in the future...

This has to be my favorite chapter in this book, which is why I saved it for last. Anything futuristic or science fiction-based is my forte. The textures presented in this chapter are a culmination of all the techniques I've demonstrated throughout this book. The images created here, as usual, utilize a combination of from scratch- and image-based texturing techniques. You can apply science fiction textures to most games, such as *Quake*, *Unreal*, or *Half-Life*. In this chapter, I'll show you how to make the following:

- A spaceship deck, complete with black and yellow caution lines, from scratch

- The spaceship deck's color palette, so a set of textures can share it to speed up game play

- Other caution line textures, created by using photographs

- Two cool sci-fi wall textures, the first created entirely from scratch using Photoshop's default tools and filters, and the second a composite image based on photographs, 3D model rendering, and Photoshop filters

tip

It's always good to have references when texturing, such as photographs of real-world objects or movies. In this chapter in particular, watch the *Aliens* movies or listen to William Orbit or Jean Michel Jarre to inspire your textures!

Spaceship Deck

This is a quick base material for any spaceship deck (or asphalt street); it will get more interesting when I show you how to add painted caution lines to the material.

1. Start a new 512 × 512-pixel RGB image.

2. For the background layer, choose Filter, Render, Clouds, using two dark gray colors as the mix. (I used hex# 212121 and hex# 343434.)

3. In the Channels palette, create a new channel.

4. To the new channel, apply Filter, Noise, Add Noise (about 50 percent).

5. To the same channel, apply Filter, Noise, Median, with a setting of 1 pixel.

6. Adjust the levels of the channel to bring out the white speckles. (See Figure 8.1.)

Figure 8.1
Adjust the levels to enhance the choppy noise.

7. To the background layer, apply Filter, Render, Lighting Effects, using the Alpha 1 map as a texture channel. (See Figure 8.2.)

Figure 8.2
Render the texture using the Alpha 1 channel as a displacement map.

Filter: Render, Lighting Effects
Light Type: Directional (vertically)
Intensity: 21
Focus: 69
Gloss: 13
Material: 50
Exposure: 18
Ambience: 21
Texture Channel: Alpha 1
Height: 100

1. Start a new channel.

2. Press Ctrl+A to select the entire channel.

3. Fill the selection with pure white.

4. Choose Edit, Stroke, and stroke the inside of the selection with pure black with a thickness of 40 pixels. (See Figure 8.3.)

Filter: Blur, Gaussian Blur
Radius: 20.0 pixels

Figure 8.4
Apply the Gaussian Blur filter to the channel.

5. Choose Filter, Blur, Gaussian Blur. (See Figure 8.4.)

6. Choose Image, Adjust, Levels, and slide the Shadows and Highlights markers toward each other until the white area has nice, crisp, round edges. (See Figure 8.5.) This is similar to applying the Threshold command.

You might want to adjust the levels again to sharpen or darken the grain in the texture. Also, there's no need to run an offset to make the texture tileable—the grain is too tight and random to make noticeable seams.

Spaceship Deck with Caution Lines

This tutorial is effective, but make sure you retain the Alpha 1 map—you'll use that to bump the paint that's been sprayed on the floor. These steps assume that you just completed the previous tutorial.

Figure 8.3
Create a new channel that has a 40-pixel border around the edges.

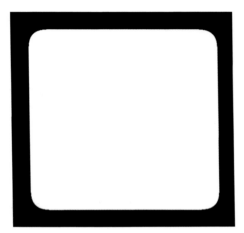

Figure 8.5
Adjust the levels or apply the Threshold command to sharpen out the channel.

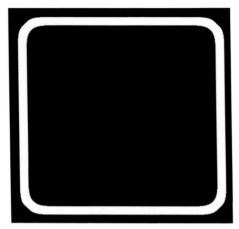

Figure 8.6
The completed white boundary that will represent the painted areas.

do so, click Edit, Transform, Rotate. Then press and hold down the Shift key and rotate the channel 45 degrees. (See Figure 8.7.)

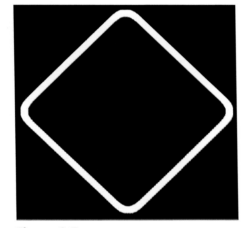

Figure 8.7
Increase the size of the canvas and rotate the channel 45 degrees.

7. Ctrl+click this channel to create the edge selection.

8. Choose Select, Modify, Expand, and enter a value of 20. Click OK.

9. Choose Select, Inverse.

10. Make sure your background color is pure white, and press Delete.

11. Press Ctrl+D to deselect.

12. Choose Image, Adjust, Invert. You should now have a white square with curved corners; this represents the painted-line

boundary that you'll apply on top of the asphalt. (See Figure 8.6.)

13. Make a copy of this channel by dragging and dropping it onto the New Channel button. This way, if you mess up the pattern, you can always revert back to the original.

14. Choose Image, Canvas Size, and change the Width and Height settings to 1024 pixels each.

15. The channel must be rotated before you can perform the diagonal cuts on the lines. To

16. Enable Photoshop's Snap and Grid functions.

17. Choose Edit, Preferences, Guides and Grid to adjust the grid settings; I placed my gridlines every 16 pixels, with only 1 subdivision. This way, selections will snap to the grid and be somewhat uniform.

18. Create a single, vertical, rectangular marquee selection that is one grid square wide, and taller than the entire image. Position it to the left, as shown in Figure 8.8.

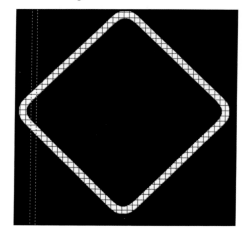

Figure 8.8
Enable the Snap and Grid features and create a single rectangular marquee selection.

19. With the first selection in place, make sure your background color is pure black and press Delete. This deletes a chunk from the white square. Continue this process all the way to the far right. (See Figure 8.9.) Notice that I left the elbows of the square intact.

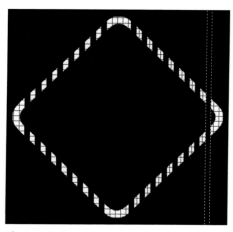

Figure 8.9
Use the marquee selection to create the "caution line" look around the white square.

20. Choose Edit, Transform, Rotate, and rotate the channel back 45 degrees.

21. Choose Image, Canvas Size, and restore the Width and Height settings to 512 pixels each.

22. Turn off the Grid feature (Ctrl+Alt+').

23. The caution-line channel is now complete. Ctrl+click this channel to load the selection. (See Figure 8.10.)

Figure 8.10
Restore the canvas and load the channel's selection.

24. With the selection loaded, go back to the Layers palette and start a new layer.

25. Fill the selection on the new layer with pure yellow (hex# FFFF00), as shown in Figure 8.11.

Figure 8.11
On a new layer, fill the selection with pure yellow.

Figure 8.12
Apply the Lighting Effects filter using the Alpha 1 map as a texture channel.

Figure 8.13
Play around with the painted lines to make them appear more worn.

26. With this layer selected, choose Filter, Render, Lighting Effects, using the same settings as before. Your texture channel should still be the Alpha 1 map. Now the painted lines take on the bumpiness of the asphalt below. (See Figure 8.12.)

You might want to make a final levels adjustment to the painted layer. Also, try changing the layer's properties to something like Hard Light to give it a worn look. In addition, apply the Spatter filter to the second Alpha channel before you load its selection;

this makes the paint appear to be chipped away. I did that, in addition to using the Eraser tool, in the image shown in Figure 8.13.

Creating a Set That Shares the Same Palette

You could make a ton of different textures based on the previous example. For instance, say that you have a spaceship deck, or many decks, that have those caution lines tracing all over the place. Maybe they're a path for a robot or something. It might be a good idea to make a nice set of tex-

tures that can be flipped and arranged to create any number of caution-line patterns. In Figure 8.14, I made six different patterns and tiled them to create a floor map.

When you create each tile, reduce the image, and then palettize the image for final import into a game, you might want to force these tiles to share the same color palette. After all, how much different are the colors between each texture? If tiles share the same palette, the game's engine can load a single palette (allowing the game to run faster). Of course, this

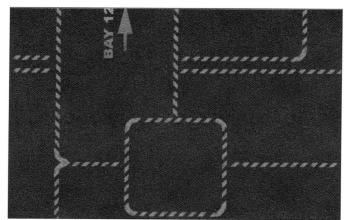

Figure 8.14
Create a tileable set of caution lines to make a variety of patterns.

applies to those engines such as *Unreal* and *Half-Life* that take advantage of shared palettes.

To see what I mean, using the previous example, click Image, Image Size, and make both the width and the height 256 pixels. Change the Resample Image setting to Bilinear to prevent a halo effect that is sometimes generated around the border of the image. Click OK. Next, palettize the image. (Click Image, Mode, Indexed Color.) Set the Colors to 256, then pull down the Palette list and select Custom. You'll get a Color Table dialog box, as shown

in Figure 8.15. Finally, click the Save button to save this palette. (Pick whatever file name you want.)

The next time you create another space-deck texture and change the mode to Indexed Color, just click Custom Palette again and load the palette you saved. The textures will share the same palette without loss of color data, and the game will be optimized.

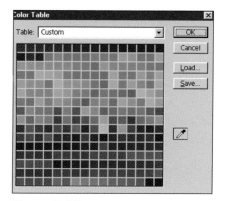

Figure 8.15
Creating a custom palette for your texture set to share.

More Caution Line-Based Textures

For some reason, the caution line thing always looks great in games—especially the futuristic ones. Because caution lines imply a sort of "Warning: Don't go in there" attitude, they entice the kid in us all to go in there anyway. Also, they're easy to create. The most important part of making caution lines is to make sure they look like scuffed, chipped paint; nobody likes a nice clean spaceship.

The next two textures demonstrate what I created using single photographs of some rusty or dirty object and used to create the rest of the image. The images were created using simple texturing techniques taught throughout this book and in the rest of this chapter. The photographs I used to create these textures are called caution1.jpg and caution2.jpg, located on the CD-ROM. See Figures 8.16 through 8.18. For the metal texture, I also incorporated the basemetal2.jpg image, which is a texture derived from the rustypanel.jpg photograph, also located on the CD.

Figure 8.16
The `caution1.jpg` photograph used to create the next texture.

Figure 8.18
The `caution2.jpg` photograph used to create the next texture.

The beveling techniques in Figure 8.19 are similar to how I create the stone wall textures in Chapter 6, "Medieval/Fantasy Textures." The metal texture portion is created from the `basemetal2.jpg` image. Again, this texture tiles only left and right and is rendered in *trueSpace*.

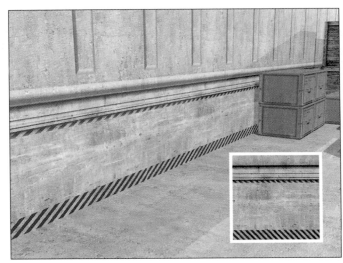

Figure 8.17
Here, I've used the cement portion of the photograph to generate a tileable caution line texture (bottom right of figure). Note that this texture tiles only on its left and right sides, and is rendered in *trueSpace 6*.

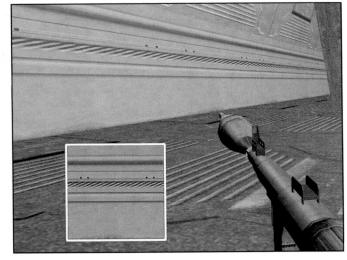

Figure 8.19
Another caution line texture, only this time over a metal surface.

Warp Core Control Center

This type of texture involves nothing less than creating lots of pipes, lights, metal panels, and anything else that makes you feel as far as possible from quaint. In addition, this texture will have an animation frame associated with it—a couple of the lights will go on and off, depending on the actions of the player (once the texture is in a game engine, that is). Figure 8.20 shows the texture whose creation I'll demonstrate now.

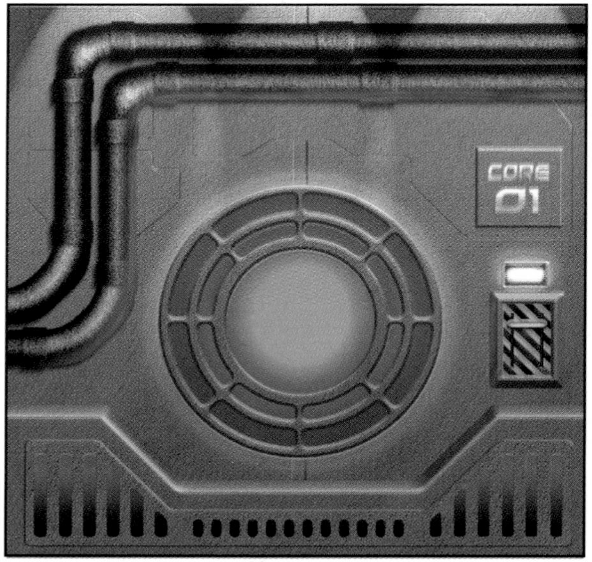

1. Start a new 1024 × 1024-pixel RGB color image with a resolution of 1024.

2. Fill the image with the Clouds filter, using pure black and medium gray (hex# 808080).

3. Choose Filter, Render, Difference Clouds.

4. Add noise, 10 percent.

5. Choose Filter, Stylize, Emboss. This makes the surface appear slightly bumpy. (See Figure 8.21.)

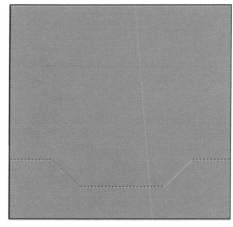

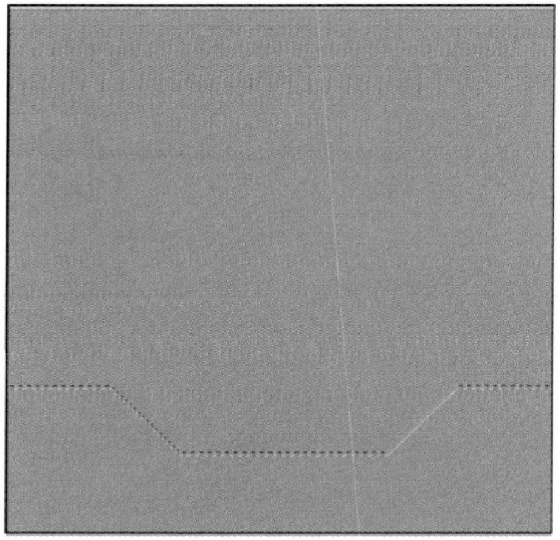

Figure 8.22
Create a polygonal selection on the background layer and copy it to a new layer.

6. Using the Polygonal Lasso tool, with both the Grid and Snap features enabled, create a selection as shown in Figure 8.22.

7. Right-click on the selection and choose Layer Via Copy.

Filter: Stylize, Emboss
Angle: 135 degrees
Height: 1 pixel
Amount: 118%

Figure 8.20
The futuristic, high-tech texture you'll create in this section.

Figure 8.21
Use the Clouds, Noise, and Emboss filters to make a uniquely textured background.

8. With the selection on its own layer, apply an inner bevel.

9. Notice that the style causes bevels on the left, right, and bottom edges, which you don't want. To get rid of them, flatten the layer (that is, add a new layer, link the two, and press Ctrl+E to merge them); click Edit, Transform, Scale; and scale out the sides and bottom.

10. Adjust the levels on all layers to darken the image. (See Figure 8.23.)

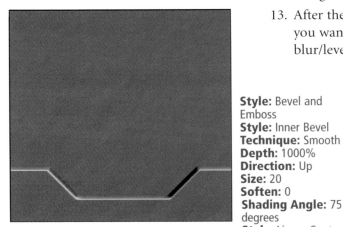

Figure 8.23
Bevel the selection based on the background texture. Adjust levels to make it darker.

11. The large, circular warp core thing (in the middle of Figure 8.20) is simply a pattern I created using an alpha channel in the Channels palette. To begin, create a circular marquee selection, and then fill it with white in a new channel.

12. Continue making the pattern by deleting and filling other circular selections, as I have done in Figure 8.24. (I used the Line tool to make the straight lines of fixed width.)

13. After the pattern is about what you want, use the Gaussian blur/levels technique, as mentioned in the previous example, to round the corners.

14. When you're finished, Ctrl+click the channel to load the selection.

Style: Bevel and Emboss
Style: Inner Bevel
Technique: Smooth
Depth: 1000%
Direction: Up
Size: 20
Soften: 0
Shading Angle: 75 degrees
Style: Linear Contour
Range: 50%

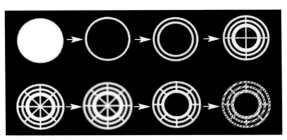

Figure 8.24
Create a cool grate pattern in a new alpha channel.

15. With the pattern's selection loaded, right-click the background layer and choose Layer Via Copy.

16. Apply an inner bevel to the new layer to make the surface look 3D. (See Figure 8.25.)

note

I don't have set preferences for bevels; I usually just play around with the settings to get the look I want. The most important thing to do is to use the Global Light feature, which is usually enabled by default.

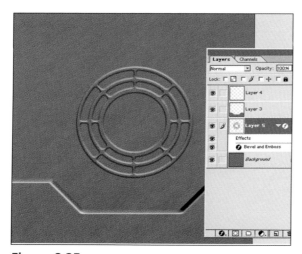

Figure 8.25
Use the pattern selection to copy the material from the background layer, and apply an inner bevel to this layer.

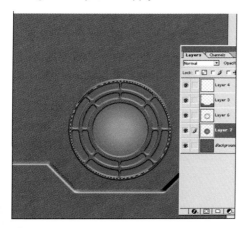

Figure 8.26
Fill a circular marquee selection with a radial gradient using black and deep red colors.

17. Start another layer below the grate.

18. Create a circular marquee selection that is almost as big as the grate; place its border right in the middle of the outside border of the grate.

19. Fill the selection with a foreground-to-background radial gradient, using black as the foreground color and a deep red, such as hex# 6F0707, as the background. You should end up with the illusion that the grate stands in front of a hot, deep warp core. (See Figure 8.26.)

20. Repeat the techniques in steps 11–14 to make another grate pattern in the same general shape as the lower portion of the wall. (See Figure 8.27.)

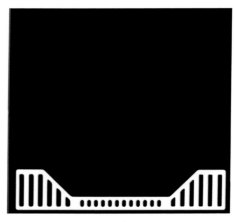

Figure 8.27
Repeat steps 11–14 to create another grate pattern for the lower portion of the wall.

21. Invert the selection, start a new layer below the grate, and fill it with a black-to-deep red linear gradient, indicating that that area is some form of vent for the warp core. (See Figure 8.28.)

22. Add an outer-glow style to the layer that contains the warp core's radial gradient. (Make sure the glow color is the same as before—in this case, hex# 6F0707.)

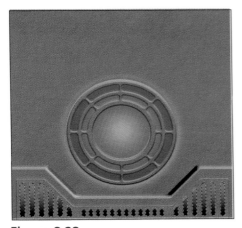

Figure 8.28
Invert the selection and fill it with a linear gradient, using the same colors as before. Add an outer glow to the radial gradient's layer.

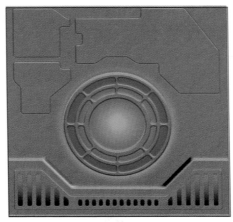

Figure 8.29
Add panels to the top portion of the background layer using Polygonal Lasso selections.

note

See the "Pipes" section in Chapter 2, "Nasty Decals," for more information about making pipes from scratch.

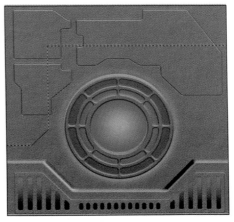

Figure 8.30
Start a pipe by making a Polygonal Lasso selection.

caution

During this tutorial, try not to flatten layers that have any type of glow styles applied to them. Near the end, you'll need to turn them on and off to simulate the texture animation during gameplay.

23. Break up the top portion of the background layer a bit by creating Polygonal Lasso selections; making a copy of that portion of the background layer; and applying a small, downward, outer bevel to them. In Figure 8.29, I created my general patterns and rounded the corners using an alpha channel and the blur-levels technique.

24. Now for the pipes that run a course through the texture: With Photoshop's Grid and Snap features enabled, create a Polygonal Lasso selection as I have done in Figure 8.30.

25. In a new alpha channel, stroke the selection with white, entering 25 for the pixel width.

26. Apply the Gaussian Blur filter to the channel, and then tighten it up again with the levels command. This smoothes out the edges.

27. Ctrl+click the channel and reapply the Gaussian Blur filter.

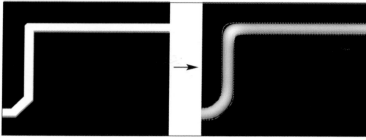

Figure 8.31
Stroke the selection in a new channel, and use the blur/levels technique to create the pipe.

copying the selection, and pasting it back into the scene. Then just scale the small piece so that it's slightly larger than the pipe to give the illusion of a collar.

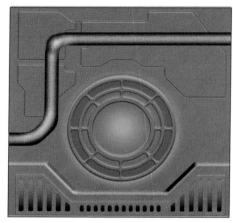

Figure 8.32
The new pipe copied over from the Alpha channel.

28. Adjust the levels a bit to make the 3D pipe come into focus. (See Figure 8.31.) (Note that this is the same technique used in Chapter 6's example of creating the medieval castle door's drop handles.)

29. Copy and paste the pipe from the Alpha channel to a new layer.

30. Apply noise (about 10 percent), and adjust the levels to darken the image and bring out the pipe's highlights. (See Figure 8.32.)

31. Create collars on the pipe by making a Rectangular Marquee selection around a small portion of the existing pipe,

32. After all the pieces have been added, merge them to the pipe's layer.

33. Add a drop shadow to the pipe. Make sure the lighting direction is the same as the bevel styles— that is, the shadow drops down and away to the left a bit. (See Figure 8.33.)

34. Make a copy of the pipe's layer and move it so it's right next to the original. The copy's edges won't be long enough, so just make a Rectangular Marquee selection around the long end, copy it, and position it to make the pipe run off of the image.

35. The portion of the pipe that's closest to the warp core could

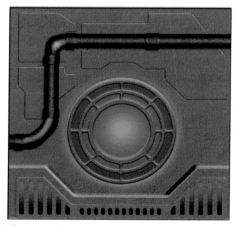

Figure 8.33
Make collars using copies of a small portion of the existing pipe. Drop-shadow the whole thing when finished.

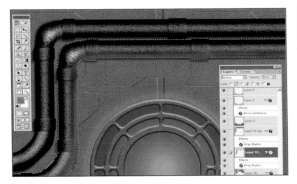

Figure 8.34
Copy the pipe and move it next to its parent. Add a bit of red glow to the bottom pipe to simulate reflectance of the warp core.

use a little reflective glow underneath it. Ctrl+click the pipe's layer to select it, and then use the Airbrush tool with a low setting (such as 3 percent) to brush in a deep red along its length. (See Figure 8.34.)

36. Make a hidden copy of this pipe so that when the lights are off, you can recall the copy to get rid of the glow.

37. Next, make an on/off panel that a player could approach and activate. In the image shown in Figure 8.35, I simply made a rectangular selection, copied a portion of the background

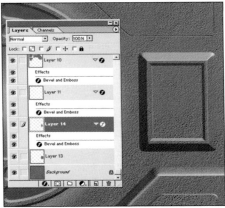

Figure 8.35
Create a raised panel using rectangular selections of the background layer and applying bevels to them.

layer, and applied an inner bevel to it just like the lower front portion of the wall. Then I added another smaller panel, this time with a downward inner bevel. The combination makes for a raised panel with another that's inset.

38. Ctrl+click the top-most beveled panel to reload its selection.

39. Fill the selection with a dirty yellow color and add a bit of noise.

40. Change the Blending Mode of this layer to Hard Light. This allows you to retain much of the color and bring out the texture of the panel behind it.

41. Adjust the levels to enhance the panel.

42. Use the Line tool to create black diagonal stripes across the selection. (Enabling Photoshop's Snap and Grid features helps this procedure.) Hold down the Shift key while making the lines to keep them at 45-degree angles. (See Figure 8.36.)

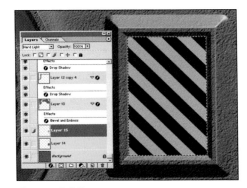

Figure 8.36
Make a caution-style texture on the top-most panel using a medium-yellow background with black lines.

43. Create another layer on top of the panel.

44. Make two black vertical lines and apply an inner bevel to both. These serve as the rails for the on/off switch.

45. Make a handle using the pipe technique described earlier. Round the ends of the handle and paste it into position.

46. Choose Image, Adjust, Variations to change the color of the handle to red. (See Figure 8.37.)

47. Add a drop shadow to the handle to pull it away from the panel.

note

Keep the handle on a separate layer so that you can move it down to the "off" position later.

48. Make an illuminated light that represents the "on" state of the entire texture. To begin, create a small rectangular panel, as before, based on the background.

49. On a new layer (above the rectangular panel), fill the inside of the panel with a reflected gradient, using medium-light blue and white foreground and background colors. (See Figure 8.38.)

50. Enhance the light by adding some light gray horizontal lines, and then go over the light with the Dodge tool until the center and edges are fairly white.

51. Use the Burn tool to darken the edges, making the light appear almost rounded and 3D.

52. Apply a blue outer glow to the light, as shown in Figure 8.39. (As with the handle you made before, keep this layer intact with its style so that you can hide the style later, making the system appear to be off.)

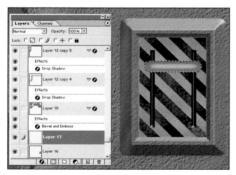

Figure 8.37
Make rails and a red handle to complete the panel.

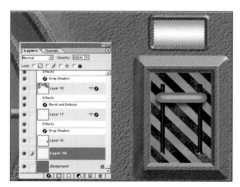

Figure 8.38
Create another small panel for the on/off light. Fill the inside with a blue-to-white reflected gradient.

Figure 8.39
The completed light, after dodging and burning here and there. An outer-glow style makes it appear to be "on."

Figure 8.40
The "off" and "on" states of the texture. A video game will call one of two different textures depending on the player's actions.

small glow, indicating that the warp core is hot but not at full power. (See Figure 8.41.)

53. Create an "off" state for the light—this is simply another layer just below the light, but filled with a deep blue gradient. In Figure 8.40, you can see the difference between the "off" state and the "on" state.

54. Now it's all a matter of creating two textures—one for when the glows are on, and one for when they're off. For the warp core's "off" state, simply hide the original red texture, create another layer, and fill it with a

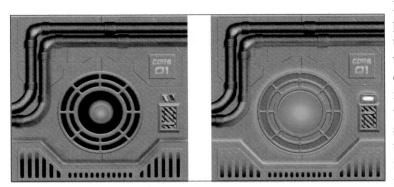

Figure 8.41
Create two textures for the final output: one with all glows turned down or off and the red handle moved down, and one with the handle up and everything lit.

Sci-Fi Wall Texture

This will be the last texture I'll show you in this book, and by far the most advanced. It embraces and enumerates just about every texturing technique I know of, and if you're able to make such a digital image, you can create textures for anything. It is a composite texture built from a single photograph of a rusty metal panel, along with a 3D model of a hose with bellows. (See Figure 8.42.)

There's quite a bit happening in this texture, and personally I wouldn't recommend creating something like this for a single wall panel in a video game. Rather, I am presenting this tutorial to you with the intent of demonstrating everything you should be able to perform when having fun with game texturing. I'm

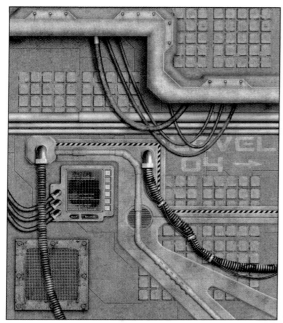

Figure 8.42
The wall texture I'll be creating in this section.

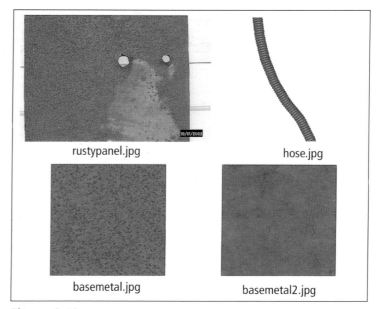

Figure 8.43
The `rustypanel.jpg`, `hose.jpg`, `basemetal.jpg`, and `basemetal2.jpg` files that will be used to create the entire texture.

also going to generalize each step of the process; however, if you've followed along from the beginning of this book, you shouldn't have problems performing any one step.

The two files I've used to create the texture are called `rustypanel.jpg` and `hose.jpg`, both of which are located on the CD-ROM. The first is the same disgusting panel I've been using from

time to time throughout this book as a base texture; it will be the source of creating the base texture of most objects in this tutorial. The second is a rendered 3D model of a hose I created in trueSpace. The hose model will serve as some cool conduits here. Finally, there are three helper files (also on the CD-ROM) that you can use if you follow along, called `basemetal.jpg`

and `basemetal2.jpg`, which are extrapolations from portions of the `rustypanel.jpg` image for creating the base metal foundations of most objects in the texture, and `console.psd`, which is a metal computer console screen with buttons that I made completely from scratch in Photoshop. (See Figure 8.43.)

1. The new image dimensions I'll be using to begin this texture are substandard to all the textures I've been teaching throughout this book, only because my original intent with this texture was to generate cover art (7.375" × 9.125"). Feel free to start off with any dimensions you like; however, to get the most detail, begin with a high resolution and a large canvas setting. Here, I'm starting with a new image at the aforementioned size (which converts to 2213 × 2738 pixels), with a resolution of 300 dpi. (That's huge! There's just over 17 MB blank!) This is maximum cover art resolution. Most printers only need 150 dpi, but working at this obese file size provides the greatest image detail. I've created a pattern from a portion of the rustypanel.jpg image and tiled it on the background of this new image. Then I've dodged a few areas here and there to break up the monotony. (See Figure 8.44.)

Figure 8.44
A large image of about 7.3" × 9.1" at 300 dpi is filled with a patternized portion of the rustypanel.jpg image.

2. To further add to the background pattern, on a separate layer I've tiled another background pattern sample based on rustypanel.jpg (see basemetal2.jpg on the CD-ROM) and set this layer's blending mode to Overlay. This is a common technique I use to generate good base textures. Next, in Chapter 4, "Military Textures," I detailed creating polygonal, raised panels off a base metal texture. Here, in Figure 8.45, I've enabled the Grid and Snap modes of Photoshop and used the Polygonal Lasso tool to create panel sections based on the background image. After creating the selections of the background layer, I copied these areas to their own layers and applied Inner Bevel styles to them. This is a panel-based pattern for the background texture. Then I adjusted the overall levels and hue/saturation to suit.

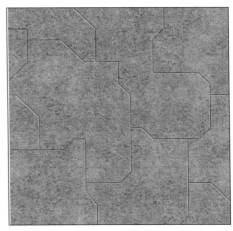

Figure 8.45
Here, I've created inset panel patterns based on the background. (See Chapter 4.) I've enlarged a portion of the image and lightened the texture so that it is visible in print.

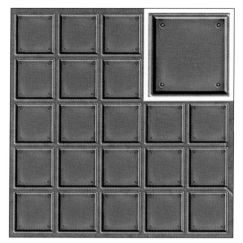

Figure 8.46
I'm creating a grid of square button-like objects that will make a nice background noise for the overall texture.

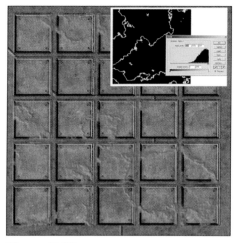

Figure 8.47
Using the lightning bolt creation technique from Chapter 3, I deleted portions of the grid to weather it.

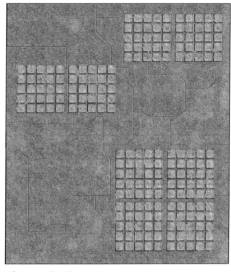

Figure 8.48
Copies of the grid are placed around the texture.

3. Next, I'm creating more background noise by creating a square selection, filling it with a reddish Clouds filter combination, and beveling it to raise it. I've added some small indented rivets for the corners, merged the layers for it, and then duplicated the object to a 5 × 5 grid. (See Figure 8.46.) The upper-right corner shows a close-up of this object.

4. Remember how I showed you how to create lightning bolts in Chapter 3, "Sprites" (Figure 3.4)? Here, I did the same thing and then loaded the lightning bolt selection and used it to partially delete portions of the grid squares, making them appear weathered. (See Figure 8.47.) Finally, I adjusted the colors a bit and added noise.

5. In Figure 8.48, I've placed several copies of the grid in various places on the texture.

6. The center portion of the texture from Figure 8.42 shows some sort of flat metal support paneling that begins at an electrical junction box and spills to the right and downward. It contains a black and yellow warning strip, similar to the textures

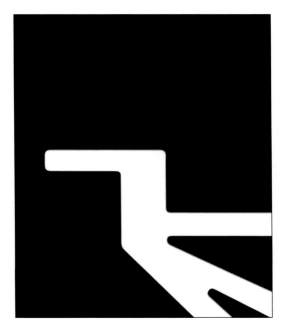

Figure 8.49
A metal support panel comes to life when you create its shape in a new channel.

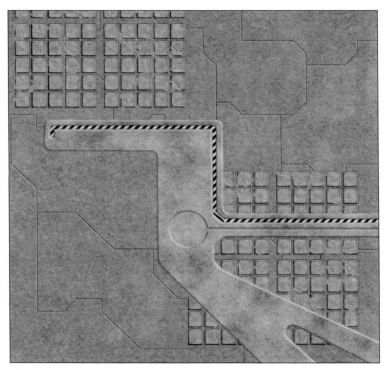

Figure 8.50
The support paneling is added by filling the selection with the `basemetal2.jpg` texture. A warning strip and another inset bevel pattern are also added.

created earlier in this chapter. The paneling supports a conduit pipe and hose and contains a vent that sports dripping rust. To begin, I created the paneling in a new channel using the Polygonal Lasso tool. Then I smoothed the edges using the Gaussian Blur/Levels technique

I've taught throughout the book. (See Figure 8.49.)

7. Using this new channel pattern, I loaded its selection and filled it with the `basemetal2.jpg` texture. (This texture was sampled

from the portion of the `rustypanel.jpg` image, mainly the portion where there was less rust and more metal.) After adjusting the colors, I added an Inner Bevel style to raise it off the background. A warning strip and another inset bevel pattern are also added. (See Figure 8.50.)

8. In the middle of the support paneling is a texturing favorite of mine—a vent with dripping rust. I think you can find something like this in every 3D game. I made the one in Figure 8.51 by creating a circular selection above the support paneling, copying its texture to a new layer, and diligently adding inner vent slats horizontally throughout the vent. I beveled each slat so that they appear to slant inward. The entire vent is laid upon a black background to give it good depth. I crowned the whole thing off by applying dripping rust, using the same dripping decal procedure I taught in Chapter 2.

9. Next, I created a conduit pipe directly from the panel texture below it. I created this pipe and its elbow joints in the same way I showed you earlier in this chapter. I also applied a drop shadow to the pipe to give it

Figure 8.51
I created a vent with dripping rust by creating a circular selection from the support paneling and adding beveled slats. The rust was created in the same way that I showed you in Chapter 2.

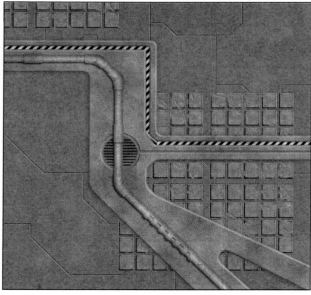

Figure 8.52
A conduit pipe is created using the panel texture directly below it.

some height, and dodged the top ridge to reflect the scene's general lighting. (See Figure 8.52.)

10. Here, I terminated the conduit pipe with an electrical junction box. The box was an octagonal pattern created in a new channel and then filled on a new layer with the `basemetal2.jpg` texture. To create the box, I

applied an inner bevel to it, flattened that layer, and then applied an outer bevel to force this object to be more 3D-like. Finally, corner rivets and a drop shadow were added to complete the effect. (See Figure 8.53.)

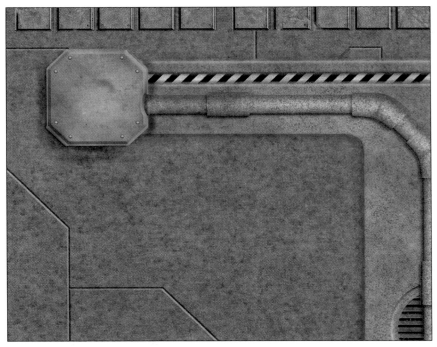

Figure 8.53
I've terminated the upper-left portion of the conduit pipe with an electrical junction box texture, made by beveling an octagonal selection that was filled with the `basemetal2.jpg` texture.

11. In the 3D modeling program trueSpace, I created a bellowed, flexible-like hose that I thought would look cool being piped out of the junction box. Creating a hose like this in Photoshop is entirely possible, but in cases like this, you'll save a ton of time making it in 3D and then pasting the image into your texture. This common practice is called *compositing*. The rendered model is located on the CD-ROM called `hose.jpg`. Here, I've created an elbow joint, as I did with the joints on the conduit, and pasted the hose beneath it. (See Figure 8.54.) To make the hose look dirty, I loaded the hose's selection, started a new layer, and applied the Clouds and Difference Clouds filters. This layer's blending mode was then set to Soft Light. I do this often

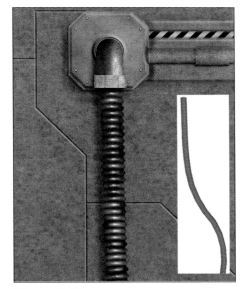

Figure 8.54
Here, I've created an elbow joint and added a hose texture. I created the hose (see `hose.jpg` on the CD-ROM) in the 3D modeling program trueSpace.

to dirty up objects in this texture.

12. Next, I added another elbow joint and hose to the metal panel. I also put in a small black wire bound by metal straps along the hose; I made the wire by creating a selection using the Path tool, stroking the path with black, and turning it into a miniature pipe using the pipe technique shown earlier in this chapter. (See Figure 8.55.)

13. The top portion of the overall texture has some sort of air conditioning duct, water main, or what have you. I made this with two different pipe layers created in separate alpha channels. The channel for one of these ducts is seen in the upper-right portion of Figure 8.56. The design, of course, is just some goofy, random pattern I made in a new channel using the Polygonal Lasso tool. Then I filled the pattern with the same basemetal2.jpg texture. (This texture image goes far, doesn't it?) To round out the large duct, I Gaussian Blurred the inner selection of the alpha channel pattern, pasted it on top of the duct on a new layer, and changed the layer's blending mode to Overlay. Dodging and burning the inside and outside of the duct rounds it off even more. Finally, I applied drop shadows and rivets with dripping rust.

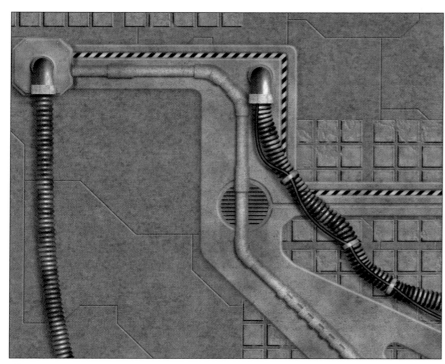

Figure 8.55
Another hose is added to the metal panel, this time coupled with a small drooping wire, created using the Path tool. The wire is a miniature version of the pipe technique.

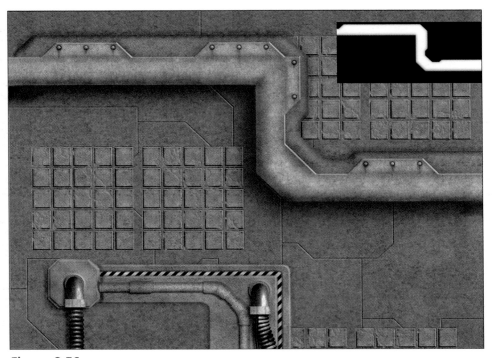

Figure 8.56
Pipe-like ducts are added to the top portion of the texture. These are just two overlaid images created in separate alpha channels and filled with the `basemetal2.jpg` texture. A large drop shadow is applied to the bottom, making both ducts float high above the overall texture.

14. To the center of the texture, I quickly added several thick pipes running straight across the image. (See Figure 8.57.) Again, the `basemetal2.jpg` texture fills them, only this time I've adjusted the colors to make them stand a bit more unique from the rest of the objects in the image. The couplings in the middle of the largest pipe add a nice touch.

15. I think every good sci-fi wall needs an indication as to which level the player is in. Here, I've added some text, whose layer's color is a deep yellow and the opacity is about 37 percent. As usual, I've chipped the edges using the Quick Mask/Spatter technique I taught in the first military panel texture in Chapter 4. (See Figure 8.58.)

16. Here's a nice touch: I've added drooping cables from the vent pipes that extend beyond the right side of the image. This is accomplished by using the Path tool to draw curved lines that simulate the pull of gravity. The path is stroked with black, and once again the pipe technique is used. I overlaid the cables with a noise layer to give them more of a rubbery look. (See Figure 8.59.) Drop shadows are applied to pull the cables away from the wall.

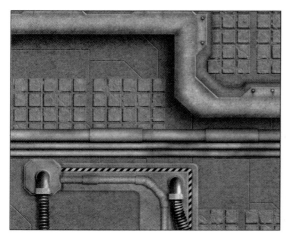

Figure 8.57
Simple thick pipes are added to the center of the texture. The pipes' colors are altered and lightened slightly to offset them from the rest of the image. Drop shadows are added as well.

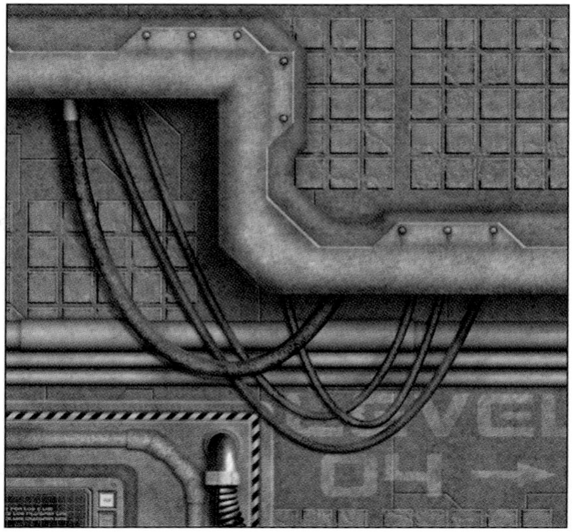

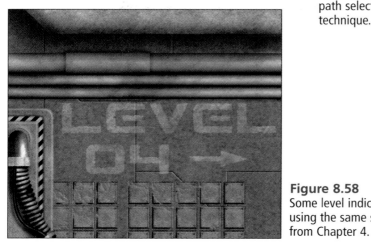

Figure 8.58
Some level indication text is added using the same spattering technique from Chapter 4.

Figure 8.59
Here, I've added black power cables hanging from the large vents. You can create them by stroking a path selection and following the same pipe creation technique.

17. To complete the texture, I've added computer console and large vent objects to the lower-left corner of the image. The console is multiple beveled panels overlaid on top of one another. You can find it on the CD-ROM as `console.psd`. The conduit hoses are the same as the drooping ones created earlier. (See Figure 8.60.)

Of course, this texture didn't evolve for me in 17 steps; it took a couple days and around 10 hours of work. And, every time I come back to it after a long break, I want to change something about it. You can make a few final adjustments, such as adding an Adjustment layer on top of all the layers, such as a Levels or Curves Adjustment layer. Also, to make the

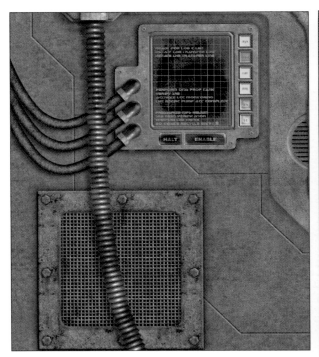

Figure 8.60
A computer console with conduit hoses and a large grated vent are added to the scene to complete the image. You can find the console object on the CD-ROM as `console.psd`.

image appear more photo-real, I flattened the entire image and applied the Auto Levels command. (See Figure 8.61.) I've saved the full texture, with all the images' objects on separate layers, on the CD-ROM and named it

Figure 8.61
The final texture, with the Auto Levels command applied. This command quickly converted the image to make the scene almost photo-real.

`Dark Side.psd`. It's a rather large file, typical of print work. When you print it at high-resolution settings on your color printer, using glossy photo paper, it looks totally cool and has a professional textbook-cover quality.

Summary

As you saw in this chapter and in examples throughout the book, you can create textures by hand, using only the default set of filters and tools contained within Photoshop, or by using a couple of decent and appropriate photographs of real-world materials, such as rusty metal. A composite texture was produced here as well. You learned to create a texture using combination techniques: texturing from scratch, using Photoshop's default filters; using photographs of rusty metal to create the base textures for many objects in the same image; and finally, importing a rendered 3D object to help save time and provide more realism to generating such a complicated texture object.

If you can create all the textures I've presented to you in this book, you can create any texture for any game. If you would like to contact me regarding any of the textures in this book or to ask other questions, please e-mail me at g_lok434@earthlink.net or visit my Web site at http://www.g-lok.com to see the rest of my artwork. I wish you the best of luck in your game art development endeavors!

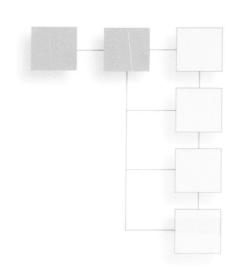

APPENDIX A

A 2D GRAPHICS PRIMER

Let's look at the basic graphic unit of an image: the *pixel* (short for *picture element*). Windows displays images on your screen in terms of pixels—rows and columns of miniscule "dots," each square shaped with varying color, that form an image. The higher the number of pixels per inch, the sharper the image becomes.

Assume you have an archaic monitor and video card that can show only one pixel on the screen, in black and white (almost like my first video game in the 70s!). The resulting image on the screen would have a *resolution* of one pixel across the first row and one pixel down the first column, or 1 × 1, as shown in Figure A.1. Also, because you can display that pixel only in black or white (that is, monochrome), the *color depth* of that single pixel would be one bit.

When it comes to pixels, each one on your screen has an assigned color depth in terms of bits. In computers, a single bit has 2^1 (or two) different states—on and off, hence the use of the binary system. (Everything is a power of two.) In the case of the pixel in Figure A.1, the on state could be

Figure A.1
A single-pixel monochromatic image.

white, and the off state could be black. All in all, you would call the video settings of this scenario 1 × 1, one bit (two color).

Obviously, you can't do much of anything with a single-pixel monitor (aside from making a large dot blink annoyingly), so you'll have to increase your resolutions and color depths to make things a tad more viable. Look at Figure A.2. As you can see, each frame increases the resolution by a power of two, in attempts to make the image sharper. The color depth, however, remains one bit.

About Bit-Processing Speeds

Frequently you'll hear about 8-, 16-, 32-, 64-, and 128-bit this, that, and the other. Although people use these terms with abandon, not everybody knows what they mean. Computers are based on binary, where all numbers are a power of two. The Central Processing Unit (CPU) of the console or personal computer is designed by engineers to process programming instruction sets (such as game code) using these numbers as the length, in terms of bits per instruction, of game code that it cranks through every cycle.

So, as you play a game, if the machine you're playing on is, say, 64-bit, then for every computer cycle (each time the data is pumped through the system per second), the CPU processes an instruction that is 64 bits in length. This might seem a bit (no pun intended) confusing, but it just means the higher the bit number, the faster the machine. Likewise, the faster the machine, the more complex graphics, sound, and general game code it can handle. You'll also see these bit capabilities applied to other things like sound and video cards.

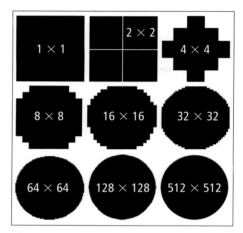

Figure A.2
The higher the resolution, the sharper the image.

Granularity and Aliasing

Granularity refers to the way the human eye can perceive all the minute details in an image. My brother Andrew, who happens to be a superb optometrist, explained to me that the total number of photoreceptors per square millimeter in the retina determines your *acuity*. When you view an object or image, the higher your acuity, the better you can differentiate the details. When it comes to images on your computer screen, the granularity of the image is directly proportional

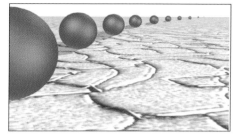

Figure A.3
Granularity of distant images.

to your acuity. In Figure A.3, for instance, as the spheres continue into the horizon, they become more and more like just a dot rather than a sphere. The granularity of the image allows your eye to perceive only so much detail at that distance.

In video games, granularity is an important concept when you work with different *Levels of Detail* (LODs) in your images. As for textures, most game engines automatically create different LODs for your images, called *mipmaps*, that are displayed at increasingly higher resolutions

depending on your physical proximity to them. Figure A.4 shows a base 256 × 256 wall texture I created, and the subsequent seven different mipmaps that were created by the *Unreal* engine. As my game character gets closer to the wall on which this texture is displayed, the engine automatically swaps the texture with its higher resolution counterpart.

Your monitor has a finite number of pixels that can be displayed per square inch (5,184 to be exact), and these pixels are generally shaped like squares. If you zoom into an image,

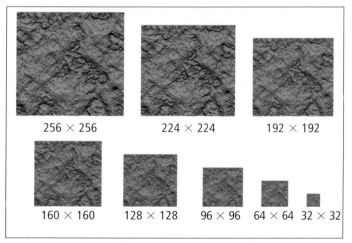

256 × 256   224 × 224   192 × 192

160 × 160   128 × 128   96 × 96   64 × 64   32 × 32

Figure A.4
Relatively sized mipmaps of a texture that is generated by a game engine.

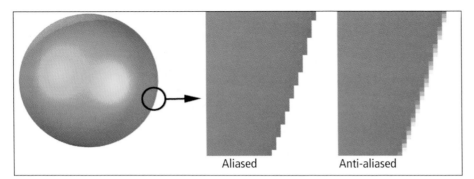

Figure A.5
An aliased and an anti-aliased image.

note

The primary colors are well known in the art world as being the fundamental *light* color set, in that with rays of light (in our case, from our monitors), you can produce any other color in the world using combinations of red, green, and blue. You see, the primary colors are additive in nature; as you add these colors together, you get other colors, and when you put all three together, you get white. (See Figure A.6.)

the edges and other details that you would expect to be smooth become *staircased*—that is, choppy and step like. This physical display limitation is known as *aliasing*. To correct aliasing and make the image appear smooth, a program can anti-alias the image. *Anti-aliasing* is a technique in which the program looks at the edge detail of an image, combines the average of the colors between the two, and fills in the gaps to make it appear smooth when you zoom out. (See Figure A.5.) Anti-aliasing is a frequently used feature in Photoshop that helps sharpen images. It's also used with 3D programs during render time to make them appear crisp.

RGB Color Depth

When computers were in their early stages, the video output was solely monochromatic. As time passed, however, people quickly became bored with monochromatic images and decided to produce monitors and video cards that could display color. To display pixels in color, electrical and computer engineers had to figure out a way to allow each pixel in an image to represent various combinations of the three primary colors: red, green, and blue.

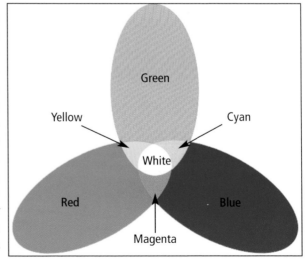

Figure A.6
The additive nature of primary colors.

So with your original 1×1, one-bit model, you need to expand both the monitor and the video card to accept an RGB color format. You can tell the engineers to make a monitor that is capable of displaying any shade of red, green, and blue on your single pixel, but you'll have to make a critical adjustment on the video card. A one-bit video card has only a single bit of memory to store the state of the pixel on the screen. If you want any of the three basic colors to be displayed, including white, you'll just double the memory to two bit so that you can store these colors. Two bits will have 2^2, or four, possible combinations. (See Figure A.7.) It's like setting switches—whatever bit combination

you set in the video card, the monitor displays that color to the screen.

I hope you can see where this is going—if you again increase the bit capability by another factor of two in your video card, you'll have a four-bit card that is capable of displaying 2^4, or 16, colors. As you increase to eight bit, or 2^8, your card will be able to hold 256 different colors—which brings up a special scenario: the Color palette.

The Color Palette

Depending on how they are designed, most monitors nowadays are capable of displaying an image resolution of 1024×768 pixels or higher on the screen at one time. When it comes to

color depth, images that have 256 (eight-bit) colors are structured using header information that contains an index and a Color Look-Up Table (CLUT). This means that each pixel in the image can have only one of 256 different colors, and the program reading the image uses the index to determine what color each pixel will have by referencing the table. (See Figure A.8.) Viewing an image with only 256 colors, however, won't properly reveal its intrinsic nature. (Photoshop works best at color modes higher than 256 anyway.) By increasing the color depth again to 16 bit, you enable the image to use 2^{16}, or 65,536, different colors. That said, it would be cumbersome and ungainly for an image file to have a CLUT capable of containing that many colors. So, the graphics designers put their thinking caps back on and came up with the concept of color channels.

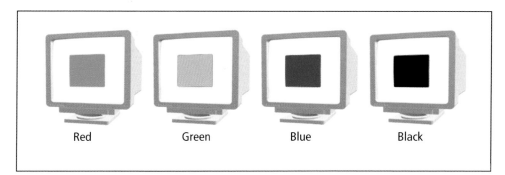

Red   Green   Blue   Black

Figure A.7
A two-bit, four-color scenario.

Pixel #8,473
has this color
at index 103

Eight-bit (256 color) image   Image's CLUT palette

Figure A.8
Eight-bit CLUT.

The highest available color depth in Windows is the ultra-true color mode, or 32 bit. The extra eight-bit portion of the pixel that's added to the 24-bit sequence is typically used as an alpha channel. This channel represents the *transparency* of a pixel; as an example, in video games, you might have seen an object break into pieces all over the floor and then slowly vanish. The programmers use this channel to diminish the colors of the pixels in the images until they are completely transparent. Then they remove the image entirely from the video card to save on memory.

RGB Color Channels

One solution to the problem of having an overwhelmingly large CLUT is to separate the red, green, and blue components into eight-bit *channels*. When an image is separated into these channels, each color can contain 2^8, or 256, different brightness levels. Because RGB color properties are additive, an image can composite the three channels to form one 3×8 or 24-bit image, where each resulting pixel in the image can have one of 2^{24}, or 16,777,216, different colors—more than enough to display the true color of an image. (See Figure A.9.) In Photoshop, you can view an image's color and alpha channels in the Channels palette.

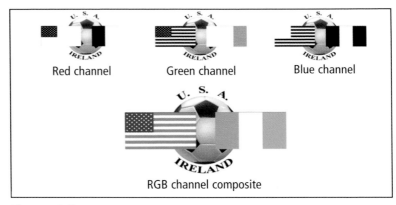

Red channel   Green channel   Blue channel

RGB channel composite

Figure A.9
The RGB color channel composite.

Video Memory

Modern video cards, particularly those designed for playing video games, have three main components: a Graphics Processing Unit (GPU), which takes care of things like world and model transformations, lighting, clipping, and rendering; *buffers,* which are special memory areas that contain either the actual image you see on your screen (the *primary* buffer) or images waiting to be flipped to the primary buffer; and Video Random Access Memory (VRAM).

Your concern is more with the VRAM, which is the area where games store all the wonderful textures and video sequences that you create. For example, when you walk around in a 3D video game, all the textures, models, and animations that aren't visible but are required for the level in which you are located are stored temporarily in VRAM. As you progress to other levels, you might see the game hesitate, or receive a message that it is "loading." In this case, the game engine is queuing up the next batch of textures, sequences, and whatnot for display in VRAM.

What all this means to you is that when you create textures, models, and animations, you need to consider optimizing each for memory. After all, it will be a while before you have video cards with 10 GB! Table A.1 covers the video memory allocation needed for various image and monitor resolutions and bit color depths.

As you can see, the higher the pixel's bit depth and the larger the dimensions of your image, the more memory the image eats up in the video card.

Later on, you'll create your images and then optimize them to take up minimal space in memory.

You might also notice that the first seven entries in Table A.1 are equal multiples of 16. As a game artist, you will typically need to create textures with image sizes divisible by 16. Can you guess why? As I discussed before, computers are based on the binary system, and video resolutions and color depths are based on this as well. Game programmers design their

Table A.1 Video Memory Allocations

Image Resolution	Bit Color Depth	VRAM Requirement
16 × 16	16, 24, 32	512 bytes, 768 bytes, 1 KB
32 × 32	16, 24, 32	2 KB, 3 KB, 4 KB
64 × 64	16, 24, 32	8.2 KB, 12.3 KB, 16.4 KB
128 × 128	16, 24, 32	32.8 KB, 49.2 KB, 65.5 KB
256 × 256	16, 24, 32	131.1 KB, 196.6 KB, 266.2 KB
512 × 512	16, 24, 32	524.3 KB, 786.4 KB, 1.1 MB
1024 × 1024	16, 24, 32	2.1 MB, 3.9 MB, 5.2 MB
Monitor Resolution	**Bit Color Depth**	**VRAM Requirement**
640 × 480	16, 24, 32	614.4 KB, 921.6 KB, 1.2 MB
800 × 600	16, 24, 32	960 KB, 1.4 MB, 1.9 MB
1024 × 768	16, 24, 32	1.6 MB, 2.4 MB, 3.1 MB

game engines around this system, so making your images in this fashion allows them to fit easily within the game engines' parameters.

tip

> To quickly figure out the size of your image, multiply the width, height, and depth (in bytes). Remember: There are eight bits in a byte, so a 1024 × 768, 24-bit image would be 1024 × 768 × 3 bytes, or 2,400 KB (2.4 MB).

A great example of these texture size restrictions is *Half-Life*. The developers of *Half-Life* put a ceiling on their textures so that the maximum dimensions of any image were 256 × 256 pixels with an eight-bit (256 color) palette. The texture is usually created at something like 512 × 512 at 24-bit color, and then reduced to this range. As technology increases, however, and better video cards and computers become available, game developers will allow higher and higher quality images. In fact, games like *Unreal Tournament* allow up to 1024 × 1024 texture resolutions, but they are typically scaled down dynamically during gameplay to 256 × 256 due to video hardware restrictions.

Other Color Modes

You have been focusing primarily on the RGB color model, which is the most versatile for game graphics, but there are a few other modes:

- CMYK
- Grayscale
- LAB

CMYK

Often, you'll see the *C*yan, *M*agenta, *Y*ellow, and Blac*k* (CMYK) mode. If you refer to the RGB color plate in Figure A.6, you will see that the intersections of these colors additively create the CMY colors. Printers usually use the CMYK colors due to their *subtractive* properties; unlike the RGB colors, which are based on light waves, CMY ink colors blend to subtractively make other colors. When all three colors are brought together, they make black. (See Figure A.10.)

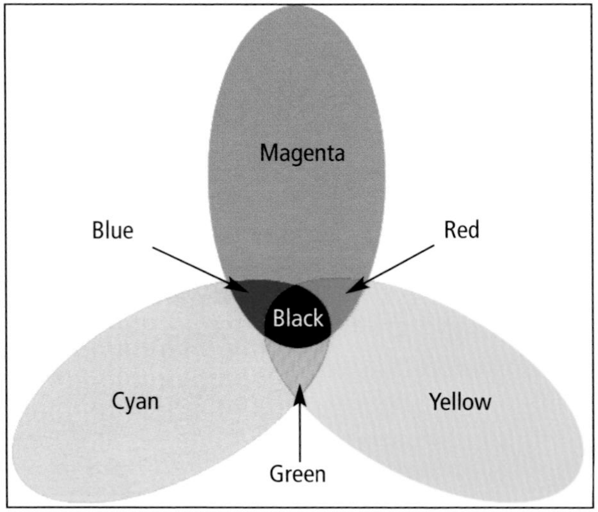

Figure A.10
The subtractive nature of the CMYK color model.

It was found, however, that when bringing equal amounts of cyan, magenta, and yellow together, the resulting mix didn't produce true black. That's why an additional black component (K) is tagged along with the other three colors whenever black is required. If you have a color printer, you can see this in action—open the lid and look at the ink cartridges. Your printer will probably have a CMY unit and a black unit. And when you're printing white? Well, just don't print anything at all!

Grayscale

Grayscale is simply an eight-bit color mode that contains 256 different shades of gray, from white to black. (See Figure A.11.) The uniqueness of a grayscale image is that it's not indexed like an eight-bit color image; rather, it has only one color channel of black, and the pixels in the image channel are based on 256 different intensities of black.

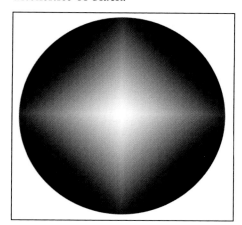

Figure A.11
A grayscale gradient image.

LAB

LAB images have three channels like RGB, but the first is a lightness channel and the other two are chromacity (color information) channels (A and B). The advantage of the LAB format is more for medium transportation purposes—if you view a LAB image onscreen, technically no color information will change when it goes to the print shop. Also, Photoshop uses LAB as an intermediary when converting from, say, RGB to CMYK, to suppress color loss. You don't need to be concerned about this; it's just good to know.

File Formats

I'm going to wrap up this appendix with some of the primary image formats you'll be using when saving your work. Each file format offers different techniques of saving image information, content, and compression. Your file-format options are as follows:

- PSD
- BMP
- JPEG
- PNG
- TGA
- TIFF

PSD

The default image format in Photoshop is PSD. When you're creating an image, all the components of the image—such as layers, styles, channels, paths, and so on—are stored in the PSD file. *Always* save your original work in this format first, and then save to another format. If you don't save your image as a PSD but need to go back to make a modification, you'll simply open a flattened image without the original components.

BMP

This is the Windows bitmap file, capable of supporting 8-, 16-, or 24-bit images. Some games, such as *Half-Life*, use this format in 8-bit mode, which is based on a 256 color palette. Typically, you create an image in 24-bit color mode; when you save it as a BMP file, the colors in the image are palettized to 8 bit. Basically, in a game, having a 24-bit image is overkill, so having your images converted to 8 bit displays enough colors for the player not to notice—at least for now.

JPEG

This is the Joint Photographic Experts Group (JPEG) file format, invented primarily for optimizing file sizes for things like the World Wide Web. The JPEG format is usually the least desirable nowadays

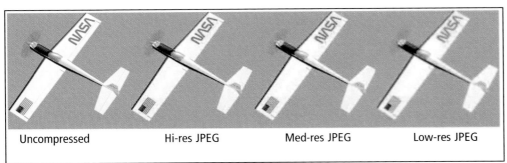

| Uncompressed | Hi-res JPEG | Med-res JPEG | Low-res JPEG |

Figure A.12
JPEG image degradation as compression increases.

because it offers variable compression settings that seriously degrade the quality of an image. (See Figure A.12.) Use this format only when you need to send pictures over the Internet.

PCX

This popular format was developed by ZSOFT as a proprietary format for their PC Paintbrush program back in the good ol' DOS days. PCX has a better compression ratio than BMP while retaining the same image quality. The *Unreal* and *Unreal Tournament* engines use this format.

PNG

The Portable Network Graphics (PNG) format is one of the best ways to preserve image data and have compression at the same time. I'm not sure why PNGs aren't used more often; this graphics format has lossless, high compression with the capability of storing alpha (transparency) information. This format was designed to replace the popular GIF format and be seamlessly portable between computer systems. GarageGames' Torque engine makes use of the PNG format.

TGA

The Targa format, developed originally for the Truevision video board, is used often when saving animation frames in 3D programs due to the high-quality image content–to-compression ratio. TGAs also store layers and transparency channels and are used within the *Quake* engine for images requiring transparency information.

TIFF

The Tagged Image File Format (TIFF) is another high-quality image format that allows for the storage of layers and transparency, just as with PSD files. The down side is TIFF's compression; TIF files, although containing high quality, usually have huge file sizes.

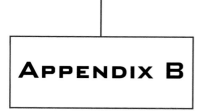

Appendix B

Photoshop Keyboard Shortcuts

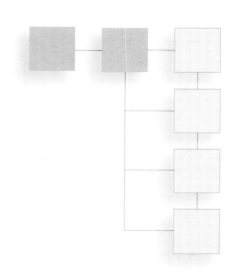

The following tables represent many—but not all—of Photoshop's keyboard shortcuts. Unless you're weirdly obsessed with Photoshop, I wouldn't recommend trying to memorize them all. In fact, the first table contains the bulk of the shortcuts that I use most often. I recommend at least being proficient with them to make your work go more quickly.

My Most Frequently Used Shortcuts

Action	Shortcut
Copy	Ctrl+C
Cut	Ctrl+X
Deselect	Ctrl+D
Fill with foreground color	Alt+Backspace
Hand tool	Spacebar, with most other tools
Merge layer down	Ctrl+E
Move tool	Ctrl, with most other tools
New canvas	Ctrl+N
New canvas with previous settings	Ctrl+Alt+N
Paste	Ctrl+V
Quick mask	Q
Repeat filter	Ctrl+F
Select all	Ctrl+A
Select layer opacity	Ctrl+click on layer
Step backward	Ctrl+Alt+Z
Step forward	Ctrl+Shift+Z
Toggle cursor shape	Caps Lock
Toggle grid	Ctrl+Alt+'
Toggle snap	Ctrl+;
Undo	Ctrl+Z

File Menu Shortcuts

Action	Shortcut
New	Ctrl+N
New document with previous settings	Ctrl+Alt+N
Open	Ctrl+O
Open as	Ctrl+Alt+O
Close	Ctrl+W
Close all	Ctrl+Shift+W
Save	Ctrl+S
Save as	Ctrl+Shift+S
Save as copy	Ctrl+Alt+S
Save for Web	Ctrl+Alt+Shift+S
Print options	Ctrl+Alt+P
Page setup	Ctrl+Shift+P
Print	Ctrl+P
Exit	Ctrl+Q
Color settings	Ctrl+Shift+K
Preferences	Ctrl+K

View Shortcuts

Action	Shortcut
Apply zoom	Shift+Enter
Fit to screen	Ctrl+0
Toggle extras	Ctrl+H
Toggle grid	Ctrl+Alt+'
Toggle guides	Ctrl+'
Toggle lock guides	Ctrl+Alt+;
Toggle menu bar	Shift+F
Toggle rulers	Ctrl+R
Toggle screen mode	F
Toggle snap	Ctrl+;
View actual pixels	Ctrl+Alt+0
Zoom in	Ctrl++
Zoom out	Ctrl+-

Toolbox Shortcuts

Action	Shortcut
Airbrush	J
Blur	R
Burn	O
Crop	C
Dodge	O
Eraser	E
Eyedropper	I
Gradient	G
Hand	H
History brush	Y
Lasso	L

Toolbox Shortcuts

Action	Shortcut
Magic wand	W
Marquee	M
Move	V
Notes	N
Paintbrush	B
Path component selection	A
Pen	P
Quick mask mode	Q
Shape	U
Sharpen	R
Slice	K
Smudge	R
Sponge	O
Stamp	S
Standard mode	Q
Type	T
Zoom	Z
Cycle tools	Shift+tool letter
Decrease brush size	[
Increase brush size	]
Decrease brush pressure	Shift+[
Increase brush pressure	Shift+]
Previous brush	<
Next brush	>
Tool opacity	1 through 9, 0
Default colors	D
Switch colors	X

Editing Shortcuts

Action	Shortcut
Cut	Ctrl+X
Copy	Ctrl+C
Copy merged	Ctrl+Shift+C
Paste	Ctrl+V
Paste into	Ctrl+Shift+V
Paste outside	Ctrl+Alt+Shift+V
Undo move	Ctrl+Z
Step backward	Ctrl+Alt+Z
Step forward	Ctrl+Shift+Z
Fade	Ctrl+Shift+F
Transform	Ctrl+T
Transform again	Ctrl+Shift+T
Fill with foreground	Alt+Backspace
Fill with background	Ctrl+Backspace
Repeat last filter	Ctrl+F
Liquify	Ctrl+Shift+X
Extract	Ctrl+Alt+X

Selection Modification Shortcuts

Action	Shortcut
Deselect	Ctrl+D
Reselect	Ctrl+Shift+D
Select all	Ctrl+A
Delete selection	Backspace, Del
Feather	Ctrl+Alt+D
Invert	Ctrl+Shift+I
Move selection 1 pixel	Ctrl+ ↑, ↓, ←, →
Move selection 10 pixels	Shift+ ↑, ↓, ←, →

Palette Display Shortcuts

Action	Shortcut
Toggle actions	F9
Toggle all palettes	Shift+Tab
Toggle color	F6
Toggle information	F8
Toggle layers	F7
Toggle toolbox and palettes	Tab

Layer Modification Shortcuts

Action	Shortcut
New layer	Ctrl+Shift+N
Layer via copy	Ctrl+J
Layer via cut	Ctrl+Shift+J
Go up a layer	Alt+]
Go down a layer	Alt+[
Move layer to top	Ctrl+Shift+]
Move layer up	Ctrl+]
Move layer down	Ctrl+[
Merge down	Ctrl+E
Merge visible	Ctrl+Shift+E
Group with previous	Ctrl+G
Change layer opacity	1 through 9, 0
Preserve transparency	/

Channel Modification Shortcuts

Action	Shortcut
Load mask as selection	Ctrl+Alt+~
Select channel	Ctrl+1 through 9
Select layer mask in channel	Ctrl+\
Toggle channel view	~

Color Modification Shortcuts

Action	Shortcut
Auto contrast	Ctrl+Alt+Shift+L
Auto levels	Ctrl+Shift+L
Color balance	Ctrl+B
Curves	Ctrl+M
Desaturate	Ctrl+Shift+U
Gamut warning	Ctrl+Shift+Y
Hue/saturation	Ctrl+U
Invert	Ctrl+I
Levels	Ctrl+L

Blending Mode Shortcuts

Action	Shortcut
Normal	Alt+Shift+N
Dissolve	Alt+Shift+I
Behind	Alt+Shift+Q
Multiply	Alt+Shift+M
Screen	Alt+Shift+S
Overlay	Alt+Shift+O
Soft light	Alt+Shift+F

Blending Mode Shortcuts

Action	Shortcut
Hard light	Alt+Shift+H
Color dodge	Alt+Shift+D
Color burn	Alt+Shift+B
Darken	Alt+Shift+K
Lighten	Alt+Shift+G
Difference	Alt+Shift+E
Exclusion	Alt+Shift+X
Hue	Alt+Shift+U
Saturation	Alt+Shift+T
Color	Alt+Shift+C
Luminosity	Alt+Shift+Y
Threshold	Alt+Shift+L
Clear	Alt+Shift+R

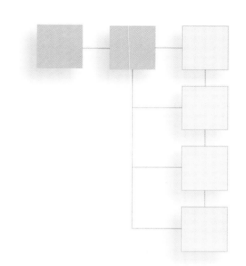

APPENDIX C

RELATED WEB SITES AND LINKS

Following is a listing of a number of my favorite sites, some of which are dedicated to textures/texturing and others to game mods, hardware, and software resources. Of course, there are a billion other texturing sites out there, but just visit this handful, and I guarantee you can find links to a plethora of other juicy sites.

Texturing Sites

As you peruse these sites, you'll come across examples that gave me so many of the ideas and tutorials I've presented in this book.

Digital Art

http://digitalart.org

This is an astounding site dedicated to the serious digital artist. It's geared more toward the freehand painter type, but you can find great examples of digital texture ability here. You'll definitely want to become a member of this site. Check out the sci-fi images, too; they inspired some of my alien skin textures.

Eyeball Design

http://www.eyeball-design.com

This site features top-quality tutorials for creating cool interfaces, textures, and Web graphics with Photoshop. It's nicely done.

GR Site's Absolute Archive

http://www.grsites.com/textures

This is a huge archive of freely downloadable, general base textures. Just make sure to get permission before you use any of the textures in a game.

Mars Global Surveyor Image Gallery

*http://www.msss.com/
moc_gallery/index.html*

Here is a mass database of images taken by the Mars Surveyor a while ago. It's a bit complex and scientific, but you'll find tons of real Martian surface images for use in texturing. After you click on an area of Mars in the maps section, just click on any one of the tiny blue streaks to obtain a high-res photo of the surface.

NASA Planetary Data System

http://pds-imaging.jpl.nasa.gov/

Some of the texturing tutorials in this book involved images of the Moon and Mars, downloaded from this site. This is another huge image database from NASA, encompassing detailed passes of these heavenly bodies as well as other planets such as Venus and the moons of Jupiter.

Ransom Active

http://www.ransomactive.com/

If you weren't happy creating your own textures and want to get your hands on some top-quality ones, this site has them for sale at a low price. Textures are seamlessly tileable and include matching bump maps. Diffusion and Alpha maps are also included with some of the textures. (But my tutorials were so fun and easy...)

Shane Caudle's Web Site

http://www.planetshane.com

Shane Caudle is the awesome lead artist on Epic Games' team, the creators of the *Unreal* series. So many of my textures are inspired by this guy; this is Shane's site, where he shows you a bunch of his 2D and 3D work, including skin tutorials.

Undulation

http://www.planetunreal.com/ undulation/

This site is the essence of *The Dark Side of Game Texturing*. You'll find lots of grueling, sinister, malicious, and twisted textures here.

Wasted Youth

http://www.wastedyouth.org

Here is a huge listing of great Photoshop tutorials for both texturing and Web design. I believe some of these examples have found their way into Eyeball Design, and some have inspired my work in this book.

Map/Mod/Level Design

Beyond the scope of this book (and subject for another book entirely!) are the areas of modifying existing games on the market to create your own, but more importantly is a way to put your textures into 3D gaming action. Here you'll find sites dedicated to mods and level designing in general, geared more toward games like *Quake*, *Half-Life*, and *Unreal*. But, you won't have to look far to find the same information for other games.

3D Map Realm

http://3dmr.gamedesign.net

3D Map Realm contains an extensive collection of *Quake*, *Half-Life*, and *Unreal* maps. There are loads of map-creation articles and discussion forums here, too.

Modpages

http://www.modpages.com

Modpages is packed with mods, mod reviews, discussions, game reviews, and the like.

Planet Half-Life, Planet Quake, and Planet Unreal

http://www.planethalflife.com

http://www.planetquake.com

http://www.planetunreal.com

By GameSpy Industries, these sites are probably your number-one source for files, utilities, maps, mods, skins, and other resources for these games. You'll probably go blind just trying to get through all their juicy details.

UnrealFiles

http://www.unrealfiles.com

UnrealFiles features a good selection of utilities and skins and an excellent link list to other sites related to *Unreal*, *Quake*, and *Half-Life*.

Unrealized

http://www.unrealized.com

You have to see this site. It's packed with great tutorials, expert advice, level-design articles, scripting tutorials—you name it. In fact, I recommend you start with this site to absorb level-editing techniques (after you've finished with this book, that is). It has a cool layout, as well.

Valve ERC

http://www.valve-erc.com

If you're hooked on *Half-Life* like I am and want all the goodies for making mods for this game, do yourself a favor and inhale the Valve ERC site. It's got it all and then some, with lots of tutorials and resources.

Graphics Software

The sites listed next are the sources of all the software used in this book, plus additional vendors of well-known 2D and 3D graphics programs.

Adobe Systems Incorporated

http://www.adobe.com

This is the site for Adobe, the creators of Photoshop, which is the best texture-creation and image-editing program in the world. Incidentally, Adobe is also the creator of Illustrator, Acrobat, Premiere, AfterEffects—jeez, it never stops! You can download trial versions of their software from this site, along

with plug-ins and documentation. You can also buy Adobe software directly from this site; Photoshop 7 runs around $600.

Jasc Software

http://www.jasc.com

Jasc Software is the creator of Paint Shop Pro, a leading yet inexpensive (just $100) 2D texture and image-editing program.

Graphics Hardware

You can't run your software without the proper computer hardware, right? Here are some key vendors of graphics hardware that usually put out the hottest video cards on the market for gaming and other hardware for graphics applications.

ATI Technologies

http://www.ati.com

ATI Technologies is the creator of the Radeon 9800 3D graphics video board ($399), featuring 128 MB of video memory, with SmartShader and SmoothVision technologies that allow for advanced full scene anti-aliasing

and anisotropic filtering, and supporting DirectX 9.

nVidia

http://www.nvidia.com

nVidia makes the GeForce4 and FX chips, which feature the nFiniteFX II engine with a 256-bit graphics core. Dual Vertex Shaders process more than 100 million vertices per second and are 50 percent faster than the previous GeForce3. The GeForce 4 also supports DirectX 9.

Wacom

http://www.wacom.com

One of the leading graphics-tablet manufacturers in the world, Wacom makes tablets that range from 4 × 5 inches for $200 to 12 × 18 inches for $700. These tablets can greatly increase the speed and quality of your 2D artwork by allowing you to draw naturally on a digitizing surface.

General Gaming and Information

These links guide you to some popular gaming forums where you can meet other developers, download gaming files, and feel generally right at gaming home.

Blue's News

http://www.bluesnews.com

Demos, patches, articles...this site keeps you current on the news in the gaming world.

ClassicGaming

http://www.classicgaming.com

Ever wanted to relive those awesome stand-up arcade video games from the 1980s? (Wait a minute...how old are you?) Anyway, for those of you (and me) who lost your weekly allowance on those digital enigmas, this site offers downloadable arcade emulators and the binary game files you need to play every game you enjoyed way back when.

Gamasutra

http://www.gamasutra.com

Gamasutra is the absolute fulcrum where game designers and developers meet to share their wisdom and resources. Membership is free. Need I say more?

GameDev.Net

http://www.gamedev.net

This is the best place on the Internet to learn about game development. This site pulls together thousands of game programming and design articles, forums, and files, and is frequented by well over 250,000 game developers each year.

Game Development Search Engine

http://www.game-developer.com

The Game Development Search Engine has compiled links to every game-related hardware and software manufacturer. This site points you in every gaming direction imaginable—graphics design, programming, forums—you name it.

Game Developers Conference

http://www.gdconf.com

This site is the online home of the Game Developers Conference, held every year—usually in March—in downtown San Jose, California. Use this site to register and to get information about airfare and hotels. (Warning: Every hotel room gets snapped up, so make your reservations early!) The conference kicks off with a few days of interactive workshops in every area of game development, followed by presentations by leading game-related companies of their latest and greatest stuff. If you can get yourself out there, I guarantee you'll love it. (Here's a tip: Take a drive north up First Street through Silicon Valley when you get a chance; for us computer geeks who don't live out there, it's love at first site.)

Game Developer Magazine

http://www.gdmag.com

I started buying this magazine back in 1994. Now I can't imagine not having a regular subscription. Each issue covers every aspect of the game-development world, keeping you up to date with professional tips, tricks, insights, innovations, and resources—and lots of pretty pictures, too.

GarageGames

http://www.garagegames.com

Home of independent games and game makers, this site has developed the Torque engine, one of the most popular and affordable 3D game engines on the market. This is a great site for finding work with independent game developers, as well as being able to contribute to the overall development of the Torque engine. The tutorials in this book are geared toward the Torque engine.

Premier Press Books

http://www.courseptr.com

What can I say? I've never known a publisher to release such an extensive and impressive collection of game-development books. Premier Press, coupled with game guru and leading game-programming author André LaMothe, has produced the most

complete game-development university in paperback, thoroughly covering game programming and design. You can buy all sorts of Premier Press titles on this Web site.

Xtreme Games, LLC

http://www.xgames3d.com

Created by leading game programming author and Premier Press Books' Editor André LaMothe, this site is dedicated to channeling the expertise of talented game developers, who share their products, knowledge, and ideas here. Additionally, Xtreme has founded the XGDC (Xtreme Game Developers Conference), a next-generation game-developers conference held each year at the Santa Clara, California, Convention Center. The XGDC is a grass-roots game developer conference with an affordable price, and tutorials for all skill levels. The XGDC has since been acquired by Course Technology and is now known as the Xtreme Game Developers Xpo (XGDX).

INDEX

License Agreement/Notice of Limited Warranty

By opening the sealed disc container in this book, you agree to the following terms and conditions. If, upon reading the following license agreement and notice of limited warranty, you cannot agree to the terms and conditions set forth, return the unused book with unopened disc to the place where you purchased it for a refund.

License:

The enclosed software is copyrighted by the copyright holder(s) indicated on the software disc. You are licensed to copy the software onto a single computer for use by a single user and to a backup disc. You may not reproduce, make copies, or distribute copies or rent or lease the software in whole or in part, except with written permission of the copyright holder(s). You may transfer the enclosed disc only together with this license, and only if you destroy all other copies of the software and the transferee agrees to the terms of the license. You may not decompile, reverse assemble, or reverse engineer the software.

Notice of Limited Warranty:

The enclosed disc is warranted by Course PTR to be free of physical defects in materials and workmanship for a period of sixty (60) days from end user's purchase of the book/disc combination. During the sixty-day term of the limited warranty, Course PTR will provide a replacement disc upon the return of a defective disc.

Limited Liability:

THE SOLE REMEDY FOR BREACH OF THIS LIMITED WARRANTY SHALL CONSIST ENTIRELY OF REPLACEMENT OF THE DEFECTIVE DISC. IN NO EVENT SHALL COURSE PTR OR THE AUTHOR BE LIABLE FOR ANY OTHER DAMAGES, INCLUDING LOSS OR CORRUPTION OF DATA, CHANGES IN THE FUNCTIONAL CHARACTERISTICS OF THE HARDWARE OR OPERATING SYSTEM, DELETERIOUS INTERACTION WITH OTHER SOFTWARE, OR ANY OTHER SPECIAL, INCIDENTAL, OR CONSEQUENTIAL DAMAGES THAT MAY ARISE, EVEN IF COURSE PTR AND/OR THE AUTHOR HAS PREVIOUSLY BEEN NOTIFIED THAT THE POSSIBILITY OF SUCH DAMAGES EXISTS.

Disclaimer of Warranties:

COURSE PTR AND THE AUTHOR SPECIFICALLY DISCLAIM ANY AND ALL OTHER WARRANTIES, EITHER EXPRESS OR IMPLIED, INCLUDING WARRANTIES OF MERCHANTABILITY, SUITABILITY TO A PARTICULAR TASK OR PURPOSE, OR FREEDOM FROM ERRORS. SOME STATES DO NOT ALLOW FOR EXCLUSION OF IMPLIED WARRANTIES OR LIMITATION OF INCIDENTAL OR CONSEQUENTIAL DAMAGES, SO THESE LIMITATIONS MIGHT NOT APPLY TO YOU.

Other:

This Agreement is governed by the laws of the State of Massachusetts without regard to choice of law principles. The United Convention of Contracts for the International Sale of Goods is specifically disclaimed. This Agreement constitutes the entire agreement between you and Course PTR regarding use of the software.